THE LOVE
SHAKE

THE
LOVE POETRY
OF
SHAKESPEARE

Edited with an introduction and notes by
ROY BOOTH

KYLE CATHIE LIMITED

First published in Great Britain in 1994 by
Kyle Cathie Limited
7/8 Hatherley Street, London SW1P 2QT

ISBN 1 85626 138 7

Introduction and notes copyright © Roy Booth 1994

Roy Booth is hereby identified as the editor of this
work in accordance with Section 77 of the Copyright, Designs
and Patents Act 1988.

A Cataloguing in Publication record for this title is
available from the British Library.

Typeset by DP Photosetting, Aylesbury, Bucks
Printed in Great Britain by
Cox & Wyman Ltd, Reading, Berkshire

CONTENTS

ACKNOWLEDGEMENTS

The editor is indebted to many previous editors, particularly of the *Sonnets*, and of them, John Kerrigan (New Penguin, 1986) and Stephen Booth (Yale, 1977). My former tutor, the late Colin Fletcher Williamson, first drew my attention to *Love's Labour's Lost* IV iii 57–8, and to his memory this edition is respectfully dedicated.

{ AJB: *This fair child of mine*
Shall sum my count and make my old excuse
TMB 1.9.93 }

INTRODUCTION

What sort of vow does a love poem represent? A naive love poet puts feelings into verse to give testimony to their sincerity. Readers of this volume will find numerous examples of love affirmed by a poem, as written by Shakespeare into the part of one of his characters. He delighted to show his stage-lovers equipped (as Proteus puts it in Act III of *The Two Gentlemen of Verona*) 'to tangle her desires / By wailful sonnets, whose composed rhymes / Should be full-fraught with serviceable vows'. In Jaques's 'All the world's a stage' speech in *As You Like It*, a manuscript love poem is the defining theatrical prop:

> *then the lover,*
> *Sighing like furnace, with a mournful ballad*
> *Made to his mistress' eyebrow*

Mercutio mocks Romeo with 'Now is he for the numbers that Petrarch flow'd in': the first result of being in love is production of a few – or a few hundred – sonnets.

The early comedy, *Love's Labour's Lost*, features a lugubrious and funny parade of the play's love-struck young men. They have all fallen in love after vowing not to do so, and, as the wittiest of them puts it, 'By heaven, I do love, and it hath taught me to rhyme': they have all committed their feelings to verse. The King of Navarre, Longaville and Dumain each in turn recite (see pages 5–8) their poems. Longaville in particular is dissatisfied with his effort, and concludes

> *I fear these stubborn lines lack power to move*
> *O sweet Maria, empress of my love,*
> *These numbers will I tear, and write in prose!*

Hearing this resolution, the witty Berowne responds in an aside:

> *O, rhymes are guards on wanton Cupid's hose:*
> *Disfigure not his shop.*

The terms are unfamiliar, but the comment he makes is profound. The language is drawn from costume: 'shop' is codpiece, and 'guards' are embroideries, with perhaps also the suggestion that rhymes restrain wantonness, by setting a guard on it.

The laconic aside makes an important suggestion about love poetry. Longaville sees his poem as a practical love lyric, aimed at moving Maria to love him, and if it lacks the power to move, not worth sending. Berowne's suggestion is that Longaville should preserve his verse as the necessary ornament (or confinement) of physical desire, which would at this time be unacceptable to Maria. Love poetry is part of the necessary form, distracting the lover from pursuing a physical approach too soon. 'When shall you see *me* write a thing in rhyme / Or groan for Joan?' asks Berowne sarcastically. But he has already done just these things; the audience has heard his poem read out (the comedy would require it to be done excruciatingly badly) by Nathaniel in the previous scene. He too is an embroiderer upon 'wanton Cupid'.

Love is a literary experience in Shakespeare. Lovers 'turn sonnet' (*Love's Labour's Lost* I ii 182) with alacrity. But as Shakespeare matured as a dramatist, the young men who recite rather precious verses in the early comedies are replaced by completely comic lovers who are simply not very good at verse, though full of feeling. The 'false gallop of verses' Orlando produces in *As You Like It* are an easy target for Touchstone's parody ('From the east to western Inde / No jewel is like Rosalind' and the rest of it turning into such buffoonery as 'Sweetest nut hath sourest rind / Such a nut is Rosalind), while Benedick in *Much Ado*, who rightly feels he was 'not born under a rhyming planet' can do no better than:

> *The god of love,*
> *That sits above,*
> *And knows me, and knows me,*
> *How pitiful I deserve.*

In still later plays, the love poetry is written into the dialogue, not set apart as the lover's composition or serenade. Troilus has no poem for Cressida, the lovers in the last plays speak with melting lyricism, but do not communicate first with paper. The last serenader is the lumpish Cloten, in *Cymbeline*, where Shakespeare exploits a comic disparity between the lover and the exquisite song he has performed (page 22).

In the end, Shakespeare would have agreed with Berowne, that even the most artless rhyme has a precious quality. But in Berowne's place Shakespeare might also have reflected that the piece of paper will retain Longaville's feelings long after he has forgotten them.

This is Shakespeare's 77th Sonnet:

Thy glass will show thee how thy beauties wear,
Thy dial how thy precious minutes waste,
These vacant leaves thy mind's imprint will bear,
And of this book this learning mayst thou taste.
The wrinkles which thy glass will truly show,
Of mouthed graves will give thee memory;
Thou by the dial's shady stealth mayst know
Time's thievish progress to eternity.

Look what thy memory cannot contain
Commit to these waste blanks, and thou shalt find
Those children nurs'd, deliver'd from thy brain,
To take a new acquaintance of thy mind.
These offices, so oft as thou wilt look,
Shall profit thee, and much enrich thy book.

Faced with the frailty of beauty and of unassisted memory, the poet invites the young man to write. A complementary sonnet (122) seems to indicate that the young man did use the book of 'vacant leaves'. Sonnet 77 is not explicitly a love poem: the tone the poet adopts is that of moral guidance. In the context, it becomes a love poem, poignant for its reticence: what the young man should memorialise by writing includes all the duties of care and forebearance towards the older man who loves him, which the other sonnets show him all too capable of forgetting.

Shakespeare's own love sonnets pass from the convinced, into self-persuasion, and eventually sharpen into the close investigations of swearing, forswearing, self-perjury and false witness we see in (to choose just two salient examples) Sonnets 138 and 152. Shakespeare, who of course was not a naive love poet, demonstrates the pained knowledge that (as his wise clown Touchstone puts it) 'the truest poetry is the most feigning, and lovers are given to poetry; and what they swear in poetry may be said as lovers they do feign'. The writer/lover necessarily 'feigns' splendid vows of constancy, for this is what convincing composition requires.

The sonnets show the difference between poetry's truer-than-true and telling the truth. Naive poetry says, 'You are fair, I say it in words as near to your beauty as I can make them'; in the end Shakespeare's own love poetry forswears its own swearing, and tells the young man, 'You are not fair' (in the sense of just) and the Dark lady, 'You are not fair' (ie. beautiful). The knowledge that poetry can misrepresent disrupts the lyric affirmations to the young man, and in the case of the dark lady supplants 'love poetry' with hyperboles of dispraise. Nevertheless what is never surrendered in these poems is a sense that poetry can make love transcend the person loved, and affirm a verity beyond the necessary verbal manipulation of its making.

The sonnets as published in 1609 are a remarkably enigmatic collection. The identities of the fair young man and the dark lady are recurrently 'discovered', but never so much as to partial, let alone universal satisfaction, despite all those promises to immortalise. What we learn about them is cumulatively to their discredit. Hardly ever has love poetry been so forthcoming about – even insistent upon – the frailties of the beloved. George Eliot could therefore turn to Shakespeares Sonnets for the epigraph to Chapter 58 of *Middlemarch*. In the novel, Lydgate is realising that he is fated to drown in the shallows of Rosamund, and the quotation used is apt to his situation:

> *For there can live no hatred in thine eye*
> *Therefore in that I cannot know thy change:*
> *In many's looks, the false heart's history*
> *Is writ in moods and frowns and wrinkles strange*

But heaven in thy creation did decree
That in thy face sweet love should ever dwell
What'er thy thoughts or thy heart's workings be
Thy looks should nothing thence but sweetness tell.

She quotes from Sonnet 93, one of Shakespeare's despairing reproaches, where captivated admiration and shocked contempt struggle for priority.

Promising to immortalise his fair friend, Shakespeare immortalised his love. In one of the most impassioned statements the sequence makes about love, Sonnet 116, love is

an ever-fixed mark
That looks on tempests and is never shaken;
It is the star to every wand'ring bark,
Whose worth's unknown, although his heighth be taken

– high, aloof, and solitary. This particular poem, epitomising an effect which is increasingly apparent in the sequence, is not poetry of union or mutuality, but poetry about love which lasts out the tempests of 'alteration' brought about by the effects of Time or the failings of the person beloved.

The sonnets concerning the 'Dark Lady' are even more disruptive of a conventional notion of love poetry. The sexuality which was ambiguously present in the fair young man poems is here overt, wonder that the face of the beloved doesn't betray his character becomes astonishment that desire should fasten on one morally polluted and undesirable to other men, ironies have toppled over into insults, quixotic self-abasement into self-degradation. The only poetry offering a comparable experience is that of Catullus about Clodia Metelli:

Odi et amo: quare id faciam, fortasse requiris,
Nescio, sed fieri sentio et excrucior.

(I hate and I love. You may ask me why I do so. I do not know, I only feel it, and it crucifies me.)

In terms of the way poets of Shakespeare's age organised their writings, this last group of poems is a paradoxical kind of palinode, a violent retraction of all the earlier amatory rhetoric. An earlier sonneteer, Thomas Watson, wrote a 'Passionate Century of Love', which at Sonnet 80 turned into a new topic: 'My Love is Past'. Often the idea of retraction is linked to a devout turning of the love to a worthier object. Shakespeare turned, though, not from love to repentance, but from love to lust, to a love less worthy, not more; though the spirit of normally palinodic poetry survives in poems like Sonnet 129 and 146.

This collection selects more than half of Shakespeare's sonnets. The sonnets urging the young man to marry, and the 'rival poet' series are the major exclusions, and poems are skipped in the sub-groupings which are chosen. With the exception of Sonnet 145, the sequence of the 1609 text is preserved. In the persuasion that the sonnets are so rich in meaning, so emotionally demanding of the leader, that nobody can really read a large number of them continuously, the sonnets here are interspersed with other texts and dramatic extracts, while some attempt is made (as far as so varied a collection of poems allows) to indicate a theme, subject or mood which is salient in the groups.

The complete text defies our attempts to know it completely. One suspects that all readers develop their own strategies of dealing with it, known routes and habitual stopping places. I hope that this substantial selection still leaves the sonnets their power to shock. If we have a sense that Shakespeare was too great a genius to be embroiled in messy human emotions, or that the main interest in his serene life was making money by means of a fluent and adaptable talent, the sonnets, written in love, written in despair, and which could never have been written for money or favour, take us aback. It is like finding oneself in a dark side street, off our familiar territory: a house is lighted, and through the partly drawn curtains there is someone we thought we knew, pleading, imploring, reproaching. The other face is unseen.

In the case of *Antony and Cleopatra*, an attempt at a fuller account of love in the play has been made, for it is the masterpiece of Shakespeare as a dramatist of love, and deserves special prominence. On the other hand, no selection is offered, nor quotations made from *Othello*. The tragic intensity of that play is perhaps measured in the way that none of the speeches can be detached from the dramatic context, from the strong individuality of Othello and Desdemona. Only more generalised lover-figures, or those lovers who, like Antony and Cleopatra, have aspects of the mythic or legendary, can be quoted in an anthology like this.

The volume is arranged into four main sections. These suggest the seasons, because Shakespeare saw love in the prospect given by Time, and his metaphorical language often makes a linkage from the various emotions aroused by love to the time of year.

The sonnets have header-quotations from the plays and narrative poems, identified at the start of the notes on the sonnet. Some are thematically connected, others are deployed as mischievous comment on the state of adulation the sonneteer finds himself recording, some are merely fanciful. Together they are meant to suggest something of the richness of Shakespeare as an aphorist on love, and how continuous his attention was to its comic absurdities and tragic power.

Poetry leads us to believe in its own potential for answering our heartbreak. We have all wanted to write a poem to express our feelings. The problem is put by Randall Jarrell, writing about 'bad poets', from the point of view of an experienced reviewer:

> In the bad type of the thin pamphlets, in hand-set lines on imported paper, people's hard lives and hopeless ambitions have expressed themselves more directly and heartbreakingly than they have ever been expressed in any work of art ... after a while one is embarrassed not so much for them as for poetry ... one finds it unbearable that poetry should be so hard to write – a game of Pin the Tail on the Donkey in which there is for most of the players no tail, no donkey.

Literature is generous to our inadequacies: we can find an expression or clarification of our feelings in the poetry we read, encouragement, or even, conceivably, release. There is no emotional copyright, so here are the writings about love by the man who (to say no more of him) always pinned on the tail just exactly right.

I

'THIS SPRING OF LOVE'

One early and two suppositious poems; extracts from Love's Labour's Lost; *a first group of sonnets; songs from the plays; extracts from* Romeo and Juliet; *and vows of love from a range of the plays.*

The poems from *The Passionate Pilgrim* serve to introduce Venus and Adonis, and the explicit sexuality reminds us that Shakespeare did not divorce love from sex. The songs recurrently use the 'seize the day' motif; impassioned pilgrims return in Romeo and Juliet's first meeting . . .

Sonnet 145

I have a sonnet that will serve the turn/To give the onset

Those lips that Love's own hand did make
Breathed forth the sound that said 'I hate'
To me that languished for her sake;
But when she saw my woeful state,   4
Straight in her heart did mercy come,
Chiding that tongue that ever sweet
Was used in giving gentle doom,
And taught it thus anew to greet: 8
'I hate' she altered with an end
That followed it as gentle day
Doth follow night, who, like a fiend,
From heaven to hell is flown away.   12
   'I hate' from HATE-AWAY she threw,
   And saved my life, saying 'not you.'

Quotation: *Two Gentlemen* III ii 93–4

Sonnet 145 from the Dark Lady sequence has recently been identified as a likely candidate for Shakespeare's earliest surviving poem. Alone among the sonnets, it uses octosyllabic lines, while its diction is simple. Although HATE-AWAY appears as 'hate away' in the 1609 text, it is capitalised here (as it might have been in Shakespeare's manuscript) to make the pun on Hathaway more apparent. Anne Hathaway was 26, and pregnant, when she married her teenaged lover in late 1582.

'The Passionate Pilgrim': two sonnets

She's love, she loves, and yet she is not lov'd

Sweet Cytherea, sitting by a brook
With young Adonis, lovely, fresh, and green,
Did court the lad with many a lovely look,
Such looks as none could look but beauty's queen.
She told him stories to delight his ear,   5
She showed him favours to allure his eye;
To win his heart she touched him here and there –
Touches so soft still conquer chastity.
But whether unripe years did want conceit,
Or he refused to take her figured proffer,   10
The tender nibbler would not touch the bait,
But smile and jest at every gentle offer.
    Then fell she on her back, fair queen and toward:
    He rose and ran away – ah, fool too froward!

Quotation: *Venus and Adonis* line 610

A sonnet from William Jaggard's bootlegged collection, *A Passionate Pilgrim* (1599 or before). Attributing the poems he printed to Shakespeare, though some were definitely not, along with versions of Sonnets 138, 144, Jaggard had poems from *Love's Labour's Lost* and a group of Venus and Adonis sonnets, perhaps written by Shakespeare around 1593, when he was writing his narrative poem, or maybe Bartholomew Griffin's miniature imitations of it. In l.14 'froward' is 'contrary', but the latent joke is on the forward and backward of sex.

My love to love is love but to disgrace it

Fair was the morn when the fair queen of love,

Paler for sorrow than her milk-white dove,
For Adon's sake, a youngster proud and wild,   4
Her stand she takes upon a steep-up hill.
Anon Adonis comes with horn and hounds.
She, seely queen, with more than love's good will
Forbade the boy he should not pass those grounds.   8
'Once,' quoth she, 'did I see a fair sweet youth
Here in these brakes deep-wounded with a boar,
Deep in the thigh, a spectacle of ruth.
See in my thigh,' quoth she, 'here was the sore.'   12
    She showed hers; he saw more wounds than one,
    And blushing fled, and left her all alone.

Quotation: *Venus and Adonis* line 412

Another of Jaggard's Venus and Adonis sonnets, too keen to be indecent to
make complete sense, but the mythological figures provide the particular
Shakespearean slant on the basic erotic principles: the reluctant youth and the
irrepressibly sexual female. 'Seely' is innocent, or worthy of compassion.
Line 2 is lacking in the early text.

Love's Labour's Lost: extracts

'Sweet Lords, sweet lovers'

Extracts from *Love's Labour's Lost*, c1593–4, Act IV scene iii. The King
of Navarre and his courtiers Longaville, Dumain and (reluctantly)
Berowne, have dedicated themselves to three year's study, abjuring the
company of women. They promptly fall in love, and predictably, start
writing love poems.

Extract one

BEROWNE *[aside]*
   By heaven, I do love, and it hath taught me to rime, and to be
   mallicholy; and here is part of my rime, and here my mallicholy.
   Well, she hath one o' my sonnets already. The clown bore it, the
   fool sent it, and the lady hath it – sweet clown, sweeter fool,
   sweetest lady! By the world, I would not care a pin if the other
   three were in. Here comes one with a paper: God give him grace
   to groan!
      He stands aside.
      The King ent'reth [with a paper].
KING Ay me!
BEROWNE *[aside]* Shot, by heaven! Proceed, sweet Cupid; thou hast
   thumped him with thy bird-bolt under the left pap. In faith, 20
   secrets!
KING *[reads]*
   'So sweet a kiss the golden sun gives not
     To those fresh morning drops upon the rose,
  As thy eye-beams when their fresh rays have smote
     The night of dew that on my cheeks down flows.
  Nor shines the silver moon one half so bright
     Through the transparent bosom of the deep
  As doth thy face, through tears of mine, give light.
     Thou shin'st in every tear that I do weep;

No drop but as a coach doth carry thee;   30
   So ridest thou triumphing in my woe.
Do but behold the tears that swell in me,
   And they thy glory through my grief will show;
But do not love thyself – then thou will keep
My tears for glasses and still make me weep.
O queen of queens, how far dost thou excel
No thought can think, nor tongue of mortal tell!'
How shall she know my griefs? I'll drop the paper.
Sweet leaves, shade folly.

Extract two

LONGAVILLE
   I fear these stubborn lines lack power to move.
   O sweet Maria, empress of my love!
   These numbers will I tear, and write in prose.
BEROWNE
   O, rimes are guards on wanton Cupid's hose;
   Disfigure not his shop.
LONGAVILLE   This same shall go.
     He reads the sonnet.
   'Did not the heavenly rhetoric of thine eye,
     'Gainst whom the world cannot hold argument,
   Persuade my heart to this false perjury?
     Vows for thee broke deserve not punishment.
   A woman I forswore, but I will prove,
     Thou being a goddess, I forswore not thee.   60
   My vow was earthly, thou a heavenly love;
     Thy grace, being gained, cures all disgrace in me.
   Vows are but breath, and breath a vapor is:
     Then thou, fair sun, which on my earth dost shine,
   Exhal'st this vapor-vow; in thee it is.
     If broken then, it is no fault of mine;
   If by me broke, what fool is not so wise
   To lose an oath to win a paradise?'

BEROWNE
　　This is the liver-vein, which makes flesh a deity,
　　A green goose a goddess. Pure, pure idolatry.　　　　　　70
　　God amend us, God amend! We are much out o' th' way.

Extract three

DUMAINE
　　I would forget her, but a fever she
　　Reigns in my blood, and will rememb'red be.
BEROWNE
　　A fever in your blood? Why, then incision
　　Would let her out in saucers. Sweet misprision!
DUMAINE
　　Once more I'll read the ode that I have writ.
BEROWNE
　　Once more I'll mark how love can vary wit.
　　　　Dumaine reads his sonnet.
DUMAINE　　'On a day (alack the day!)
　　　　　　Love, whose month is ever May,
　　　　　　Spied a blossom passing fair
　　　　　　Playing in the wanton air.
　　　　　　Through the velvet leaves the wind,　　　　100
　　　　　　All unseen, can passage find;
　　　　　　That the lover, sick to death,
　　　　　　Wished himself the heaven's breath.
　　　　　　Air, quoth he, thy cheeks may blow;
　　　　　　Air, would I might triumph so,
　　　　　　But, alack, my hand is sworn
　　　　　　Ne'er to pluck thee from thy thorn.
　　　　　　Vow, alack, for youth unmeet,
　　　　　　Youth so apt to pluck a sweet!
　　　　　　Do not call it sin in me,
　　　　　　That I am forsworn for thee;
　　　　　　Thou for whom Jove would swear
　　　　　　Juno but an Ethiop were;
　　　　　　And deny himself for Jove,

Turning mortal for thy love.'
This will I send, and something else more plain,
That shall express my true love's fasting pain.

Extract four

BEROWNE
Sweet lords, sweet lovers, O, let us embrace!
As true we are as flesh and blood can be;
The sea will ebb and flow, heaven show his face:
Young blood doth not obey an old decree.
We cannot cross the cause why we were born;
Therefore, of all hands must we be forsworn.

Extract one   Lines 11–39. The King of Navarre, ever voluble, overflows the sonnet form with a superfluous additional couplet. The sonneteers Thomas Watson and Barnabe Barnes published similar metrical oddities in their sonnet collections of 1593.

Extract two   Lines 50–71. The sonnet is reprinted in Jaggard's collection, *A Passionate Pilgrim* (1599).

Extract three   Lines 90–117. The 'ode' is reprinted in Jaggard's collection, *A Passionate Pilgrim* (1599).

Extract four   Lines 209–14. Berowne's confession that he too loves is made in the form of a sonnet's sestet.

'Lord of my love': sonnets

Will you then write me a sonnet in praise of my beauty?

Shall I compare thee to a summer's day?
Thou art more lovely and more temperate.
Rough winds do shake the darling buds of May,
And summer's lease hath all too short a date.   4
Sometime too hot the eye of heaven shines,
And often is his gold complexion dimmed;
And every fair from fair sometime declines,
By chance, or nature's changing course, untrimmed: 8
But thy eternal summer shall not fade
Nor lose possession of that fair thou ow'st,
Nor shall Death brag thou wand'rest in his shade
When in eternal lines to time thou grow'st.   12
   So long as men can breathe or eyes can see,
   So long lives this, and this gives life to thee.

Sonnet 18   Quotation: *Much Ado* V ii 3–4

The previous 17 sonnets have urged the young man to marry. The fascination of his self-absorbed sexuality has an accumulated erotic power, which precipitates into this love poem. The earlier argument disappears: made eternal by the poet's 'eternal lines' rather than what 16 had called 'lines of life', the young man is no longer threatened by time.

Then love-devouring death do what he dare

Devouring Time, blunt thou the lion's paws,
And make the earth devour her own sweet brood;
Pluck the keen teeth from the fierce tiger's jaws,
And burn the long-lived phoenix in her blood;   4
Make glad and sorry seasons as thou fleet'st,
And do whate'er thou wilt, swift-footed Time,
To the wide world and all her fading sweets,
But I forbid thee one most heinous crime: 8
O, carve not with thy hours my love's fair brow,
Nor draw no lines there with thine antique pen;
Him in thy course untainted do allow
For beauty's pattern to succeeding men.   12
    Yet do thy worst, old Time: despite thy wrong,
    My love shall in my verse ever live young.

Sonnet 19   Quotation: *Romeo and Juliet* II vi 7

The confidence of 18 is here qualified, in one of those sonnets where the fears expressed in the body of the poem are not quite balanced and cancelled by the affirmation in the couplet. The 'antique pen' is both aged, like Time, but also as in 'antique work', grotesque decoration.

the dribbling dart of love

A woman's face, with Nature's own hand painted,
Hast thou, the master-mistress of my passion;
A woman's gentle heart, but not acquainted
With shifting change, as is false women's fashion;   4
An eye more bright than theirs, less false in rolling,
Gilding the object whereupon it gazeth;
A man in hue all hues in his controlling,
Which steals men's eyes and women's souls amazeth.   8
And for a woman wert thou first created,
Till Nature as she wrought thee fell a-doting,
And by addition me of thee defeated
By adding one thing to my purpose nothing.   12
    But since she pricked thee out for women's pleasure,
    Mine be thy love, and thy love's use their treasure.

Sonnet 20   Quotation: *Measure for Measure* I iii 2

Uses 'feminine' rhymes throughout (where the rhyme is on the penultimate
syllable of each line), and is a variant on the Pygmalion story: Nature falls in
love with her own creation, and adds a 'thing . . . for women's pleasure'. To
prick out was to choose from a list, but of course identifies what Nature added.
'Hues' in l.7 was italicised as *hews* in the 1609 text, whence Oscar Wilde's
fantasy of 'Will Hughes'.

Some love of yours hath writ to you in rhyme

So is it not with me as with that Muse
Stirred by a painted beauty to his verse,
Who heaven itself for ornament doth use
And every fair with his fair doth rehearse;   4
Making a couplement of proud compare
With sun and moon, with earth and sea's rich gems,
With April's first-born flowers, and all things rare
That heaven's air in this huge rondure hems.   8
O let me, true in love, but truly write,
And then believe me, my love is as fair
As any mother's child, though not so bright
As those gold candles fixed in heaven's air: 12
    Let them say more that like of hearsay well;
    I will not praise that purpose not to sell.

Sonnet 21   Quotation: *Two Gentlemen* I ii 79

Like Sonnet 130, in comparison to the hyperbolic claims of other writers, the
poem affirms love through understatement and a refusal to flatter. 'Rehearse'
(l.4) suggests the repetitive and stock nature of the other Muse's comparisons,
'couplement' (l.5) is a joining together, 'rondure' (l.8) the whole of Creation,
'hearsay' (l.13) empty talk.

Jove knows I love; but who?
Lips, do not move: no man must know.

As an unperfect actor on the stage,
Who with his fear is put besides his part,
Or some fierce thing replete with too much rage,
Whose strength's abundance weakens his own heart;   4
So I, for fear of trust, forget to say
The perfect ceremony of love's rite,
And in mine own love's strength seem to decay,
O'ercharged with burden of mine own love's might.   8
O, let my books be then the eloquence
And dumb presagers of my speaking breast,
Who plead for love, and look for recompense,
More than that tongue that more hath more expressed. 12
   O, learn to read what silent love hath writ:
   To hear with eyes belongs to love's fine wit.

Sonnet 23   Quotation: *Twelfth Night* II v 89–92

About feeling tongue-tied in the presence of the beloved, which is compared to
stage-fright or rage turning to apoplexy. The clever l.12 plays on 'more': his
writings plead with greater earnest than a cleverer verbal expression of a larger
claim (either of more love or for more in returned affection).

Ambitious love hath so in me offended

Lord of my love, to whom in vassalage
Thy merit hath my duty strongly knit,
To thee I send this written ambassage
To witness duty, not to show my wit;   4
Duty so great, which wit so poor as mine
May make seem bare, in wanting words to show it,
But that I hope some good conceit of thine
In thy soul's thought, all naked, will bestow it;   8
Till whatsoever star that guides my moving
Points on me graciously with fair aspect,
And puts apparel on my tottered loving
To show me worthy of thy sweet respect: 12
    Then may I dare to boast how I do love thee:
    Till then not show my head where thou mayst prove me.

Sonnet 26   Quotation: *All's Well* III iv 5

The sonnet fixes an impression that the young man is the poet's social
superior. It looks back to Sonnet 23 for assertions of inadequate command of
words, so that the recipient must supply eloquence and ornament, the poem
showing duty more than the sender can show wit or dare show love. A faint
undercurrent of bawdy makes playful the subservience.

Love hath chas'd sleep from my enthrall'd eyes

Weary with toil, I haste me to my bed,
The dear repose for limbs with travail tired,
But then begins a journey in my head
To work my mind when body's work's expired;   4
For then my thoughts, from far where I abide,
Intend a zealous pilgrimage to thee,
And keep my drooping eyelids open wide,
Looking on darkness which the blind do see;   8
Save that my soul's imaginary sight
Presents thy shadow to my sightless view,
Which, like a jewel hung in ghastly night,
Makes black night beauteous and her old face new. 12
   Lo, thus, by day my limbs, by night my mind,
   For thee and for myself no quiet find.

Sonnet 27   Quotation: *Two Gentlemen* II iv 130

A sonnet combining the topics of separation from the beloved, and seeing best in the dark, when a dream of the lover presents itself. 'Travail' in l.2 is normally modernised to 'travel', but that loses the older sense, 'painful exertion'. 'Intend' (l.6) is 'set out on', but also suggests in the modern sense of the word that these thoughts are beyond control; 'shadow' (l.10) means picture.

Love, thou knowst, is full of jealousy

When, in disgrace with Fortune and men's eyes,
I all alone beweep my outcast state,
And trouble deaf heaven with my bootless cries,
And look upon myself and curse my fate,   4
Wishing me like to one more rich in hope,
Featured like him, like him with friends possessed,
Desiring this man's art, and that man's scope,
With what I most enjoy contented least;   8
Yet in these thoughts myself almost despising,
Haply I think on thee, and then my state,
Like to the lark at break of day arising
From sullen earth, sings hymns at heaven's gate;   12
    For thy sweet love rememb'red such wealth brings
    That then I scorn to change my state with kings.

Sonnet 29   Quotation: *Two Gentlemen* II iv 173

This sonnet sublimely exploits the 8/6 line division ('octave' and 'sestet')
essential to the form in Italian, but often lost in Shakespeare's 4/4/4/2 pattern.
'I', 'my', 'myself', then 'one', 'him', 'this man', 'that man' lead to the exultant
'thee'. Luck is personified in Fortune, 'men's eyes' means (in) common
opinion, 'bootless' means futile.

Nay, dry your eyes;
Tears show their love, but want their remedies

When to the sessions of sweet silent thought
I summon up remembrance of things past,
I sigh the lack of many a thing I sought,
And with old woes new wail my dear time's waste: 4
Then can I drown an eye, unused to flow,
For precious friends hid in death's dateless night,
And weep afresh love's long since cancelled woe,
And moan th' expense of many a vanished sight. 8
Then can I grieve at grievances foregone,
And heavily from woe to woe tell o'er
The sad account of fore-bemoanèd moan,
Which I new pay as if not paid before. 12
　　But if the while I think on thee, dear friend,
　　All losses are restored and sorrows end.

Sonnet 30　Quotation: *Richard II* III iii 202–3

The thought of the beloved which compensates the poet for his woes is here delayed to the final couplet (compare 29). The metaphorical language of the poem includes a summons to appear at a court in session, the loss of what was precious, and casting up (telling) accounts. 'Sight' in l.8 was a variant form of 'sigh', so the sense is both 'things once seen' and 'costly sighing'.

But I love thee; none but thee; and thou deservest it

Thy bosom is endearèd with all hearts
Which I by lacking have supposèd dead;
And there reigns love, and all love's loving parts,
And all those friends which I thought burièd.   4
How many a holy and obsequious tear
Hath dear religious love stol'n from mine eye,
As interest of the dead, which now appear
But things removed that hidden in thee lie!   8
Thou art the grave where buried love doth live,
Hung with the trophies of my lovers gone,
Who all their parts of me to thee did give;
That due of many now is thine alone.   12
　　Their images I loved I view in thee,
　　And thou, all they, hast all the all of me.

Sonnet 31　　Quotation: *Merry Wives* III iii 62–3

The sonnet develops the convention of love as an exchange of hearts: the hearts that the poet once received from previous lovers are rediscovered in the young man, while the 'parts of me' (l.11) (amounting to 'all') that he had given have also been passed on to the youth. 'Endeared' (l.1) is 'made more valuable'; 'obsequious' (l.5) tears are 'dutiful' and 'suitable for a funeral'; the modern sense, 'flattering' may also be felt.

'It was a lover and his lass': songs from the plays

Song one

Who is Silvia? What is she,
    That all our swains commend her?
Holy, fair, and wise is she;
    The heaven such grace did lend her,
That she might admirèd be.

Is she kind as she is fair?
    For beauty lives with kindness.
Love doth to her eyes repair,
    To help him of his blindness,
And, being helped, inhabits there.

Then to Silvia let us sing,
    That Silvia is excelling.
She excels each mortal thing
    Upon the dull earth dwelling.
To her let us garlands bring.

Song two

Tell me where is fancy bred,
    Or in the heart, or in the head?
How begot, how nourishèd?
    Reply, reply.
It is engend'red in the eyes,
With gazing fed, and fancy dies
In the cradle where it lies.
    Let us all ring fancy's knell.
    I'll begin it – Ding, dong, bell.
ALL   Ding, dong, bell.

Song three

> Sigh no more, ladies, sigh no more!
>   Men were deceivers ever,
> One foot in sea, and one on shore;
>   To one thing constant never.
>   Then sigh not so,
>   But let them go,
>   And be you blithe and bonny,
> Converting all your sounds of woe
>   Into Hey nonny, nonny.
>
> Sing no more ditties, sing no moe,
>   Of dumps so dull and heavy!
> The fraud of men was ever so,
>   Since summer first was leavy.
>   Then sigh not so, &c.

Song four

> It was a lover and his lass,
>   With a hey, and a ho, and a hey nonino,
> That o'er the green cornfield did pass
>   In springtime, the only pretty ringtime,
> When birds do sing, hey ding a ding, ding.
> Sweet lovers love the spring.
>
> Between the acres of the rye,
>   With a hey, and a ho, and a hey nonino,
> These pretty country folks would lie
>   In springtime, &c.
>
> This carol they began that hour,
>   With a hey, and a ho, and a hey nonino,
> How that a life was but a flower
>   In springtime, &c.

And therefore take the present time,
    With a hey, and a ho, and a hey nonino,
For love is crownèd with the prime
    In springtime, &c.

Song five

Take, O take those lips away,
    That so sweetly were forsworn;
And those eyes, the break of day,
    Lights that do mislead the morn;
But my kisses bring again, bring again,
Seals of love, but sealed in vain, sealed in vain.

Song six

AUTOLYCUS	Get you hence, for I must go
	Where it fits not you to know.
DORCAS	Whither?
MOPSA	O, whither?
DORCAS	Whither?
MOPSA	It becomes thy oath full well,
	Thou to me thy secrets tell.
DORCAS	Me too; let me go thither.
MOPSA	Or thou goest to th'grange or mill.
DORCAS	If to either, thou dost ill.
AUTOLYCUS	Neither.
DORCAS	What, neither?
AUTOLYCUS	Neither.
DORCAS	Thou hast sworn my love to be.
MOPSA	Thou hast sworn it more to me.
	Then whither goest? say, whither?

Song seven

CLOTEN I would this music would come. I am advised to give her music a-mornings; they say it will penetrate.

Enter Musicians.

Come on, tune. If you can penetrate her with your fingering, so; we'll try with tongue too. If none will do, let her remain, but I'll never give o'er. First, a very excellent good-conceited thing; after, a wonderful sweet air with admirable rich words to it – and then let her consider.

> *Song.*
> Hark, hark, the lark at heaven's gate sings,
>   And Phoebus gins arise,
> His steeds to water at those springs
>   On chaliced flowers that lies;
> And winking Mary-buds begin
>   To ope their golden eyes.
> With every thing that pretty is,
>   My lady sweet, arise,
>   Arise, arise!

Song one   Two Gentlemen of Verona (1590–1) IV ii 39–53. The exquisite simplicity of the love song is ironically complicated in its performance by the slippery Proteus (and others), ostensibly for Thurio's benefit, really for his own, wooing his friend Valentine's lady (Silvia), and overheard by his own lady, Julia.

Song two   The Merchant of Venice (1596–7) III ii 63–72. Sung while Bassanio chooses between caskets of gold, silver and lead: if he chooses wisely, he will marry Portia. The song deals with the short life of 'fancy', love based on liking what you see, rather than love born in the heart.

Song three   Much Ado About Nothing (1598) II iii 53–68. The sentiments of the song are more true than the performer (Balthazar) and his audience (Don Pedro, Claudio, Leonato) are aware of: in the plot Claudio deserts Hero when she needs his faith.

Song four   As You Like It (1599–1600) V iii 14–37. Sung by two page boys to the clown Touchstone and his partner-to-be, the goat-herd Audrey. A *carpe diem* ('seize the day') song; 'ringtime' would be a time for dancing in rings (or, some prefer, a time for giving and receiving wedding rings).

Song five   Measure for Measure (1603) IV i 1–6. Sung by a boy to Mariana, who has been jilted by Angelo. The eyes are 'break-of-day lights', mistaken for the morning.

Song six   The Winter's Tale (1609) IV iv 297–309. Performed by the ballad-seller Autolycus and the shepherdesses Dorcas and Mopsa, as he advertises it, a 'passing merry' ballad of 'Two maids wooing a man'.

Song seven   Cymbeline (1610) II iii 11–28. The clownish Cloten, stepson of King Cymbeline, tries to woo his stepsister Imogen with the assistance of music. The bawdy quibbles in his speech show his nature, but he appreciates a beautiful song. In the song, the sense is that Phoebus (the sun) begins ('gins') to arise, to water the horses which draw his chariot with the dew which lies on the flowers. 'Mary-buds' are closed marigolds.

Romeo and Juliet: extracts

Extract one

ROMEO
   If I profane with my unworthiest hand
      This holy shrine, the gentle sin is this;
   My lips, two blushing pilgrims, ready stand
      To smooth that rough touch with a tender kiss.
JULIET
   Good pilgrim, you do wrong your hand too much,
      Which mannerly devotion shows in this;
   For saints have hands that pilgrims' hands do touch,
      And palm to palm is holy palmers' kiss.
ROMEO
   Have not saints lips, and holy palmers too?   100
JULIET
      Ay, pilgrim, lips that they must use in prayer.
ROMEO
   O, then, dear saint, let lips do what hands do!
      They pray; grant thou, lest faith turn to despair.
JULIET
   Saints do not move, though grant for prayers' sake.
ROMEO
   Then move not while my prayer's effect I take.
   Thus from my lips, by thine my sin is purged.
      [Kisses her.]
JULIET
   Then have my lips the sin that they have took.
ROMEO
   Sin from my lips? O trespass sweetly urged!
      Give me my sin again.
      [Kisses her.]
JULIET   You kiss by th'book.

Extract two

ROMEO
    He jests at scars that never felt a wound.
      [Enter Juliet above at a window.]
    But soft! What light through yonder window breaks?
    It is the East, and Juliet is the sun!
    Arise, fair sun, and kill the envious moon,
    Who is already sick and pale with grief
    That thou her maid art far more fair than she.
    Be not her maid, since she is envious.
    Her vestal livery is but sick and green,
    And none but fools do wear it. Cast it off.
    It is my lady; O, it is my love!   10
    O that she knew she were!
    She speaks, yet she says nothing. What of that?
    Her eye discourses; I will answer it.
    I am too bold; 'tis not to me she speaks.
    Two of the fairest stars in all the heaven,
    Having some business, do entreat her eyes
    To twinkle in their spheres till they return.
    What if her eyes were there, they in her head?
    The brightness of her cheek would shame those stars
    As daylight doth a lamp; her eyes in heaven   20
    Would through the airy region stream so bright
    That birds would sing and think it were not night.
    See how she leans her cheek upon her hand!
    O that I were a glove upon that hand,
    That I might touch that cheek!

Extract three

ROMEO
    Lady, by yonder blessèd moon I vow,
    That tips with silver all these fruit-tree tops –

JULIET
    O, swear not by the moon, th' inconstant moon,
    That monthly changes in her circled orb,   110
    Lest that thy love prove likewise variable.

ROMEO
    What shall I swear by?

JULIET   Do not swear at all;
    Or if thou wilt, swear by thy gracious self,
    Which is the god of my idolatry,
    And I'll believe thee.

ROMEO   If my heart's dear love –

JULIET
    Well, do not swear. Although I joy in thee,
    I have no joy of this contract to-night.
    It is too rash, too unadvised, too sudden;
    Too like the lightning, which doth cease to be
    Ere one can say 'It lightens.' Sweet, good night!   120
    This bud of love, by summer's ripening breath,
    May prove a beauteous flow'r when next we meet.
    Good night, good night! As sweet repose and rest
    Come to thy heart as that within my breast!

Extract four

    Enter Juliet alone.

JULIET
    Gallop apace, you fiery-footed steeds,
    Towards Phoebus' lodging! Such a wagoner
    As Phaeton would whip you to the west
    And bring in cloudy night immediately.
    Spread thy close curtain, love-performing night,
    That runaways' eyes may wink, and Romeo
    Leap to these arms untalked of and unseen.
    Lovers can see to do their amorous rites
    By their own beauties; or, if love be blind,
    It best agrees with night. Come, civil night,   10
    Thou sober-suited matron, all in black,

And learn me how to lose a winning match,
Played for a pair of stainless maidenhoods.
Hood my unmanned blood, bating in my cheeks,
With thy black mantle till strange love grow bold,
Think true love acted simple modesty.
Come, night; come, Romeo; come, thou day in night;
For thou wilt lie upon the wings of night
Whiter than new snow upon a raven's back.
Come, gentle night; come, loving, black-browed night; 20
Give me my Romeo; and, when he shall die,
Take him and cut him out in little stars,
And he will make the face of heaven so fine
That all the world will be in love with night
And pay no worship to the garish sun.
O, I have bought the mansion of a love,
But not possessed it; and though I am sold,
Not yet enjoyed. So tedious is this day
As is the night before some festival
To an impatient child that hath new robes   30
And may not wear them.

Extract one   Romeo and Juliet (1595) I v 92–109. The first exchange between Romeo and Juliet takes the form of a sonnet, plus the first quatrain of another.

Extract two   II ii 1–25. Line 1 responds to the banter of Mercutio, and could be thought the shortest soliloquy in Shakespeare. Romeo speaks in the language of sonneteers, compare Sidney's 53rd sonnet: 'Stella . . . Who hard by made a window send forth light'.

Extract three   II ii 107–24. A moment of foreboding strikes Juliet as Romeo offers to swear he loves her.

Extract four   III ii 1–31. Juliet, alone, speaks her own epithalamion or marriage-ode, in which she looks forward to her wedding night. Lines 21–5 anticipate the ecstasy of their love: 'dying' was what Elizabethans called the sexual climax.

Love avowed: play extracts

Extract one

LYSANDER   If thou lovest me then,
    Steal forth thy father's house to-morrow night;
    And in the wood, a league without the town
    (Where I did meet thee once with Helena
    To do observance to a morn of May),
    There will I stay for thee.
HERMIA   My good Lysander,
    I swear to thee by Cupid's strongest bow,
    By his best arrow, with the golden head,   170
    By the simplicity of Venus' doves,
    By that which knitteth souls and prospers loves,
    And by that fire which burned the Carthage queen
    When the false Troyan under sail was seen,
    By all the vows that ever men have broke
    (In number more than ever women spoke),
    In that same place thou hast appointed me
    To-morrow truly will I meet with thee.
LYSANDER
    Keep promise, love.

Extract two

POLONIUS
    [Reads the] letter.
    'To the celestial, and my soul's idol, the most beautified
    Ophelia,' –   110
    That's an ill phrase, a vile phrase; 'beautified' is a vile phrase.
    But you shall hear. Thus:
        [Reads.]
    'In her excellent white bosom, these, &c.'

QUEEN
   Came this from Hamlet to her?
POLONIUS
   Good madam, stay awhile. I will be faithful.
      [Reads.]
                  'Doubt thou the stars are fire;
                     Doubt that the sun doth move;
                  Doubt truth to be a liar;
                     But never doubt I love.
      'O dear Ophelia, I am ill at these numbers. I have not art   120
   to reckon my groans, but that I love thee best, O most best,
   believe it. Adieu.
                  'Thine evermore, most dear lady,
                     whilst this machine is to him, Hamlet.'

Extract three

   HELENA   Can't no other,
      But I your daughter, he must be my brother?
   COUNTESS
      Yes, Helen, you might be my daughter-in-law.
      God shield you mean it not! 'daughter' and 'mother'
      So strive upon your pulse. What, pale again?
      My fear hath catched your fondness. Now I see
      The myst'ry of your loneliness, and find
      Your salt tears' head. Now to all sense 'tis gross:
      You love my son. Invention is ashamed,
      Against the proclamation of thy passion,
      To say thou dost not. Therefore tell me true;   170
      But tell me then, 'tis so; for look, thy cheeks
      Confess it, t' one to th' other, and thine eyes
      See it so grossly shown in thy behaviors
      That in their kind they speak it. Only sin
      And hellish obstinacy tie thy tongue,
      That truth should be suspected. Speak, is't so?
      If it be so, you have wound a goodly clew;
      If it be not, forswear't; howe'er, I charge thee,

As heaven shall work in me for thine avail,
To tell me truly.
HELENA   Good madam, pardon me.   180
COUNTESS
  Do you love my son?
HELENA   Your pardon, noble mistress!
COUNTESS
  Love you my son?
HELENA   Do not you love him, madam?
COUNTESS
  Go not about; my love hath in't a bond
  Whereof the world takes note. Come, come, disclose
  The state of your affection, for your passions
  Have to the full appeached.
HELENA [kneels]   Then I confess
  Here on my knee before high heaven and you,
  That before you, and next unto high heaven,
  I love your son.
  My friends were poor but honest; so's my love.   190
  Be not offended, for it hurts not him
  That he is loved of me. I follow him not
  By any token of presumptuous suit,
  Nor would I have him till I do deserve him;
  Yet never know how that desert should be.
  I know I love in vain, strive against hope;
  Yet in this captious and intenible sieve
  I still pour in the waters of my love
  And lack not to lose still. Thus, Indian-like,
  Religious in mine error, I adore   200
  The sun that looks upon his worshipper
  But knows of him no more. My dearest madam,
  Let not your hate encounter with my love,
  For loving where you do; but if yourself,
  Whose agèd honor cites a virtuous youth,
  Did ever in so true a flame of liking,
  Wish chastely and love dearly, that your Dian
  Was both herself and Love, O, then give pity

To her whose state is such that cannot choose
But lend and give where she is sure to lose;   210
That seeks not to find that her search implies,
But, riddle-like, lives sweetly where she dies.

Extract four

FLORIZEL   What you do
  Still betters what is done. When you speak, sweet,
  I'ld have you do it ever. When you sing,
  I'ld have you buy and sell so, so give alms,
  Pray so, and for the ord'ring your affairs,
  To sing them too. When you do dance, I wish you 140
  A wave o' th' sea, that you might ever do
  Nothing but that, move still, still so,
  And own no other function. Each your doing,
  So singular in each particular,
  Crowns what you are doing in the present deeds,
  That all your acts are queens.
PERDITA   O Doricles,
  Your praises are too large. But that your youth,
  And the true blood which peeps fairly through't,
  Do plainly give you out an unstained shepherd,
  With wisdom I might fear, my Doricles,   150
  You wooed me the false way.
FLORIZEL   I think you have
  As little skill to fear as I have purpose
  To put you to't. But come; our dance, I pray.
  Your hand, my Perdita. So turtles pair
  That never mean to part.
PERDITA   I'll swear for 'em.

Extract five

MIRANDA   Do you love me?

FERDINAND

  O heaven, O earth, bear witness to this sound,

  And crown what I profess with kind event

  If I speak true! if hollowly, invert   70

  What best is boded me to mischief! I,

  Beyond all limit of what else i' th' world,

  Do love, prize, honor you.

MIRANDA   I am a fool

  To weep at what I am glad of.

PROSPERO *[aside]*   Fair encounter

  Of two most rare affections! Heavens rain grace

  On that which breeds between 'em!

FERDINAND   Wherefore weep you?

MIRANDA

  At mine unworthiness, that dare not offer

  What I desire to give, and much less take

  What I shall die to want. But this is trifling;

  And all the more it seeks to hide itself,   80

  The bigger bulk it shows. Hence, bashful cunning,

  And prompt me, plain and holy innocence!

  I am your wife, if you will marry me;

  If not, I'll die your maid. To be your fellow

  You may deny me; but I'll be your servant,

  Whether you will or no.

FERDINAND   My mistress, dearest,

  And I thus humble ever.

MIRANDA   My husband then?

FERDINAND

  Ay, with a heart as willing

  As bondage e'er of freedom. Here's my hand.

MIRANDA
  And mine, with my heart in't; and now farewell   90
  Till half an hour hence.
FERDINAND   A thousand thousand!
          Exeunt [Ferdinand and Miranda severally].

Extract one   *A Midsummer Night's Dream* (1595) I i 163–79. The couplets in which Hermia swears to meet her lover do not exclude a moment of satire on his sex.

Extract two   Hamlet's love letter to Ophelia, read out by her father, *Hamlet* (1600–1) II ii 109–24. His verse lines, appropriately for his intellect, constitute a miniature 'metaphysical' poem, affirming certainty in the face of universal dubeity.

Extract three   *All's Well That Ends Well* (1604–5) I iii 160–212. Helena, a physician's daughter, is made to confess to the Countess her socially-inappropriate love of the Countess' son. To 'wind a goodly clew' (ie, ball of twine) was a proverbial sarcasm, 'got yourself in a mess'; 'appeached' means 'informed against you'. 'Captious and intenible' is a linguistic doubling, a 'hendiadys': a sieve is both capacious (you can go on pouring into it) and holds nothing. Helena hopes that the Countess too might have wished 'your Dian (Goddess of Chastity) Was both herself and Love' (Venus). Her final line says that her love will remain undeclared, a mystery. Helena actually pursues Bertram with all means at her disposal.

Extract four   *The Winter's Tale* (1609) IV iv 135–55. Prince Florizel, who is being watched by his father, speaks his love to Perdita, actually a princess, but brought up as a shepherd's daughter. She thinks he is trying to seduce her ('fear . . . you wooed me the false way'), which he denies.

Extract five   *The Tempest* (1611) III i 67–91. Overlooked by her father, Prospero, Ferdinand and Miranda betroth themselves.

II

'EVEN SO MY SUN ONE EARLY MORN DID SHINE'

The short summer of love: sonnets about the 'sensual fault' of the young man, forgiveness, and a subsequent renewal of the poet's love. Extracts from *Venus and Adonis*; and Henry Willobie depicting W.S. giving him robust advice on seduction. The melancholy of Shakespeare's most musical play, *Twelfth Night* follows, and a nocturne to music from *The Merchant of Venice*.

'Sons of the world may stain': sonnets

My love admits no qualifying dross

Full many a glorious morning have I seen
Flatter the mountain tops with sovereign eye,
Kissing with golden face the meadows green,
Gilding pale streams with heavenly alchemy;   4
Anon permit the basest clouds to ride
With ugly rack on his celestial face,
And from the forlorn world his visage hide,
Stealing unseen to west with this disgrace: 8
Even so my sun one early morn did shine
With all-triumphant splendor on my brow;
But, out alack, he was but one hour mine,
The region cloud hath masked him from me now.   12
　　Yet him for this my love no whit disdaineth;
　　Suns of the world may stain when heaven's sun staineth.

Sonnet 33   Quotation: *Troilus and Cressida* IV iv 9

Sonnets 33 and 34 allude to the English weather-lore, 'fine before seven, rain
before eleven' to describe the effect of the 'sensual fault' of the young man: too
glorious a morning does not guarantee a good day. 'Rack' (l.6) means a mass
of clouds, the emergent sun/son wordplay gives the poem a suggestion of
elegy.

The brains of my Cupid's knocked out

Why didst thou promise such a beauteous day
And make me travel forth without my cloak,
To let base clouds o'ertake me in my way,
Hiding thy brav'ry in their rotten smoke?   4
'Tis not enough that through the cloud thou break
To dry the rain on my storm-beaten face,
For no man well of such a salve can speak
That heals the wound, and cures not the disgrace: 8
Nor can thy shame give physic to my grief;
Though thou repent, yet I have still the loss:
Th' offender's sorrow lends but weak relief
To him that bears the strong offence's cross.   12
    Ah, but those tears are pearl which thy love sheeds,
    And they are rich and ransom all ill deeds.

Sonnet 34   Quotation: *All's Well* III ii 16

Continues the figure of 33, but breaks into bitter reproaches, despite the
youth's 'shame', the poet drawing attention to his tears (the rain of l.6), and
how the emotional wound has left a scar (l.8) until relenting in 13-14 at the
sight of the young man's tears. The couplet rhyme 'Sheeds/deeds' uses an old
variant form of 'sheds'. In l.2, 'travel' modernises the 1609 'travaile' (see note
on 27 l.2). The modern sense seems dominant here.

*What too curious dreg espies my sweet lady in the fountain
of our love?*

No more be grieved at that which thou hast done:
Roses have thorns, and silver fountains mud;
Clouds and eclipses stain both moon and sun,
And loathsome canker lives in sweetest bud.   4
All men make faults, and even I in this,
Authorizing thy trespass with compare,
Myself corrupting, salving thy amiss,
Excusing thy sins more than thy sins are;   8
For to thy sensual fault I bring in sense
(Thy adverse party is thy advocate)
And 'gainst myself a lawful plea commence;
Such civil war is in my love and hate   12
    That I an accessary needs must be
    To that sweet thief which sourly robs from me.

Sonnet 35   Quotation: *Troilus and Cressida* III ii 63

After the tears (34), forgiveness extends to the poet trying to share the blame,
but the attempt at witty generosity has too strong a sense of self-pollution; the
falsity of the 'course of nature' analogies in ll.2–4 is exposed, so the 'sour' in the
poem's tone is stronger than the 'sweet'. The 'sensual'/'sense' play in l.8 turns
on the difference between 'of the senses' and 'of the reason'.

Venus smiles not in a house of tears

Let me confess that we two must be twain
Although our undivided loves are one:
So shall those blots that do with me remain,
Without thy help by me be borne alone.   4
In our two loves there is but one respect,
Though in our lives a separable spite,
Which though it alter not love's sole effect,
Yet doth it steal sweet hours from love's delight. 8
I may not evermore acknowledge thee,
Lest my bewailèd guilt should do thee shame;
Nor thou with public kindness honor me
Unless thou take that honor from thy name: 12
    But do not so; I love thee in such sort
    As, thou being mine, mine is thy good report.

Sonnet 36 Quotation: *Romeo and Juliet* IV i 8

In this sad poem, the resistance to self-blame in 35 has collapsed into obscure self-scapegoating. The 'separable spite' (l.6) is apparently some unlucky factor in their lives keeping them apart: perhaps social distance, or even that despite their mutual feeling ('one respect'), love between two men is fated to secrecy. The last lines, to the effect that dishonour to you (by being publicly kind to me) is dishonour to me, mask a faint threat.

I know no ways to mince it in love

Take all my loves, my love, yea, take them all:
What hast thou then more than thou hadst before?
No love, my love, that thou mayst true love call;
All mine was thine before thou hadst this more.   4
Then, if for my love thou my love receivest,
I cannot blame thee for my love thou usest;
But yet be blamed if thou this self deceivest
By wilful taste of what thyself refusest.   8
I do forgive thy robb'ry, gentle thief,
Although thou steal thee all my poverty;
And yet love knows it is a greater grief
To bear love's wrong than hate's known injury.   12
    Lascivious grace, in whom all ill well shows,
    Kill me with spites; yet we must not be foes.

Sonnet 40   Quotation: *Henry V* V ii 125

The complacencies of 30 and 31 are shaken up when the young man takes the
poet's (present) mistress. 'Love' is used for the young man, the mistress, desire
and true affection. Lines 7–8 infer that the young man is being false to his own
feelings. The 'ill' that 'well shows' (l.13) both 'looks like good' and 'is all too
apparent'.

Art thou a woman's son, and can'st not feel
What 'tis to love?

Those pretty wrongs that liberty commits
When I am sometime absent from thy heart,
Thy beauty and thy years full well befits,
For still temptation follows where thou art.   4
Gentle thou art, and therefore to be won;
Beauteous thou art, therefore to be assailed;
And when a woman woos, what woman's son
Will sourly leave her till she have prevailed?   8
Ay me, but yet thou mightst my seat forbear,
And chide thy beauty and thy straying youth,
Who lead thee in their riot even there
Where thou art forced to break a twofold truth: 12
    Hers, by thy beauty tempting her to thee,
    Thine, by thy beauty being false to me.

Sonnet 41   Quotation: *Venus and Adonis* 202–3

The poet tries to reconcile himself to events: the wrongs done are appropriate
to youth, beauty, to someone socially 'gentle', to manliness, but 'beauty' and
'straying youth' (in which such acts might be excusable) are personified in
10–11 as aspects of his nature the young man might control. 'Seat' in l.9 is place
of possession.

I am he that is so love-shaked

That thou hast her, it is not all my grief,
And yet it may be said I loved her dearly;
That she hath thee is of my wailing chief,
A loss in love that touches me more nearly.   4
Loving offenders, thus I will excuse ye:
Thou dost love her because thou know'st I love her,
And for my sake even so doth she abuse me,
Suff'ring my friend for my sake to approve her.   8
If I lose thee, my loss is my love's gain,
And losing her, my friend hath found that loss:
Both find each other, and I lose both twain,
And both for my sake lay on me this cross.   12
    But here's the joy: my friend and I are one;
    Sweet flattery! then she loves but me alone.

Sonnet 42   Quotation: *As You Like It* III ii 340

The poem deals with loving and losing, and finds an unconvincing consolation based on the conceit that true lovers 'are one'. The repeated 'for my sake' and 'lay on me this cross' make the poet Christ-like in his innocence and willing sacrifice, excusing a peccant daughter of Eve and son of Adam.

How sweet is love itself possess'd
When but love's shadows are so rich in joy!

When most I wink, then do mine eyes best see,
For all the day they view things unrespected;
But when I sleep, in dreams they look on thee
And, darkly bright, are bright in dark directed.　4
Then thou, whose shadow shadows doth make bright,
How would thy shadow's form form happy show
To the clear day with thy much clearer light
When to unseeing eyes thy shade shines so!　8
How would, I say, mine eyes be blessèd made
By looking on thee in the living day,
When in dead night thy fair imperfect shade
Through heavy sleep on sightless eyes doth stay!　12
　　All days are nights to see till I see thee,
　　And nights bright days when dreams do show thee me.

Sonnet 43　Quotation: *Romeo and Juliet* V i 10–11

Shakespeare's super-witty version of the 'seeing best in the dark' topos, when dreaming of the beloved makes darkness bright (cp 27). 'Wink' is simply 'have my eyes closed'; 'shadow' is exploited in its sense of 'image' as well as 'opposite of substance' and 'darkness', so the 'shadow's form' (l.6) is the young man himself, who would make 'clearer light' (l.7) than the 'living day' (l.10).

Love is a spirit all compact of fire

If the dull substance of my flesh were thought,
Injurious distance should not stop my way;
For then, despite of space, I would be brought,
From limits far remote, where thou dost stay.   4
No matter then although my foot did stand
Upon the farthest earth removed from thee;
For nimble thought can jump both sea and land
As soon as think the place where he would be.   8
But, ah, thought kills me that I am not thought,
To leap large lengths of miles when thou art gone,
But that, so much of earth and water wrought,
I must attend time's leisure with my moan,   12
    Receiving naught by elements so slow
    But heavy tears, badges of either's woe.

Sonnet 44   Quotation: *Venus and Adonis* 149

The theory of the four elements considered all substances to combine earth, air, water and fire. In this poem of absence, 'thought' has the volatility of air and fire, but the 'dull substance' of flesh is unable to 'leap large lengths of miles' to be with the beloved. Earth and water were seen as combining to make the melancholy humour.

Fie, fie, fond love, thou art so full of fear

How careful was I, when I took my way,
Each trifle under truest bars to thrust,
That to my use it might unusèd stay
From hands of falsehood, in sure wards of trust! 4
But thou, to whom my jewels trifles are,
Most worthy comfort, now my greatest grief,
Thou best of dearest, and mine only care,
Art left the prey of every vulgar thief. 8
Thee have I not locked up in any chest,
Save where thou art not, though I feel thou art,
Within the gentle closure of my breast,
From whence at pleasure thou mayst come and part; 12
 And even thence thou wilt be stol'n, I fear,
 For truth proves thievish for a prize so dear.

Sonnet 48 Quotation: *Venus and Adonis* 1021

In l.5, understand '(compared) to whom'. While 'hands of falsehood' steal jewels, even truth would steal a possession as precious as the friend. The predictable but beautifully worked figure in 9–14 acknowledges that the youth is not the poet's possession, but at (with a faint suggestion of 'for') pleasure steals away from the poet's breast (or is stolen).

The pangs of despised love

Against that time, if ever that time come,
When I shall see thee frown on my defects,
Whenas thy love hath cast his utmost sum,
Called to that audit by advised respects;   4
Against that time when thou shalt strangely pass
And scarcely greet me with that sun, thine eye,
When love, converted from the thing it was,
Shall reasons find of settled gravity: 8
Against that time do I ensconce me here
Within the knowledge of mine own desert,
And this my hand against myself uprear
To guard the lawful reasons on thy part.   12
   To leave poor me thou hast the strength of laws,
   Since why to love I can allege no cause.

Sonnet 49   Quotation: *Hamlet* III i 72

The poet prepares for the time when his friend disowns him, and to justify the
rejection, considers (l.9) and bears witness to (ll. 11–12) his own unworthiness.
But his knowledge of his own 'desert' (which suggests 'merit' as readily as
unworthiness) is also suggested, which gives extra force to the self-pity of the
couplet. 'Ensconce' (l.9) means fortify; Shakespeare often uses the word to
mean 'take refuge in a place of hiding'.

O most potential love! vow, bond, nor space,
In thee hath neither sting, knot, nor confine.

How heavy do I journey on the way
When what I seek (my weary travel's end)
Doth teach that ease and that repose to say,
'Thus far the miles are measured from thy friend.' 4
The beast that bears me, tired with my woe,
Plods dully on, to bear that weight in me,
As if by some instinct the wretch did know
His rider loved not speed, being made from thee. 8
The bloody spur cannot provoke him on
That sometimes anger thrusts into his hide,
Which heavily he answers with a groan,
More sharp to me than spurring to his side; 12
    For that same groan doth put this in my mind:
    My grief lies onward and my joy behind.

Sonnet 50   Quotation: *A Lover's Complaint* 264–5

After the sentiments of reluctance to leave behind in 48, a sonnet about reluctant travelling away. The end of the journey offers no hope of ease, as ll. 3–4 explain.

This precious book of love, this unbound lover

So am I as the rich whose blessèd key
Can bring him to his sweet up-lockèd treasure,
The which he will not ev'ry hour survey,
For blunting the fine point of seldom pleasure.   4
Therefore are feasts so solemn and so rare,
Since, seldom coming, in the long year set,
Like stones of worth they thinly placèd are,
Or captain jewels in the carcanet.   8
So is the time that keeps you as my chest,
Or as the wardrobe which the robe doth hide,
To make some special instant special blest
By new unfolding his imprisoned pride.   12
    Blessèd are you, whose worthiness gives scope,
    Being had, to triumph, being lacked, to hope.

Sonnet 52   Quotation: *Romeo and Juliet* I iii 88

The series of absence sonnets leads to this poem which ingeniously finds a
consolation in the idea of the enhanced pleasure when he finally sees his friend.
The suggestion of a miser gloating over his wealth, and an undercurrent of
bawdy, qualify and complicate the effect.

Wonder of nature! I have heard a sonnet begin so to one's mistress

What is your substance, whereof are you made,
That millions of strange shadows on you tend?
Since every one hath, every one, one shade,
And you, but one, can every shadow lend.   4
Describe Adonis, and the counterfeit
Is poorly imitated after you.
On Helen's cheek all art of beauty set,
And you in Grecian tires are painted new.   8
Speak of the spring and foison of the year:
The one doth shadow of your beauty show,
The other as your bounty doth appear,
And you in every blessèd shape we know.   12
   In all external grace you have some part,
   But you like none, none you, for constant heart.

Sonnet 53   Quotation: *Henry V* III vii 40–2

The poem asserts that the friend is beautiful in every conceivable way, male and female, whilst everyone else has but a single 'shade' (shadow/image/style of beauty). But the distance from 'What is your substance?' to the answer, 'constant heart' is too great, and disturbing mutability is the stronger impression, so that the last line's 'Nobody is like you . . .' could rather suggest, 'You like nobody, nobody could like you . . .'.

As waggish boys in game themselves forswear
So the boy Love is perjured everywhere

O, how much more doth beauty beauteous seem
By that sweet ornament which truth doth give:
The rose looks fair, but fairer we it deem
For that sweet odor which doth in it live.   4
The canker blooms have full as deep a dye
As the perfumèd tincture of the roses,
Hang on such thorns, and play as wantonly
When summer's breath their maskèd buds discloses;   8
But, for their virtue only is their show,
They live unwooed and unrespected fade,
Die to themselves. Sweet roses do not so:
Of their sweet deaths are sweetest odors made.   12
    And so of you, beauteous and lovely youth,
    When that shall vade, my verse distills your truth.

Sonnet 54   Quotation: *Midsummer Night's Dream* I i 240–1

The poem returns to imagery used in sonnets urging the young man to marry, but the distillation of his beauty is here not in offspring, but in the poet's verse. 'Cankers' (l.5) are dog-roses, 'vade' (l.14) is a variant of 'fade', but with suggestions of 'depart'.

The strong base and building of my love
Is as the very centre of the earth

Not marble nor the gilded monuments
Of princes shall outlive this pow'rful rime,
But you shall shine more bright in these contents
Than unswept stone, besmeared with sluttish time.   4
When wasteful war shall statues overturn,
And broils root out the work of masonry,
Nor Mars his sword nor war's quick fire shall burn
The living record of your memory.   8
'Gainst death and all oblivious enmity
Shall you pace forth; your praise shall still find room
Even in the eyes of all posterity
That wear this world out to the ending doom.   12
    So, till the judgment that yourself arise,
    You live in this, and dwell in lovers' eyes.

Sonnet 55   Quotation: *Troilus and Cressida* IV ii 102–3

The claim of poetry to immortalise had, classically, been that it conferred
immortality on the poet. Shakespeare confines the effect to his subject – yet the
process still depends on the poet, and the sonnets notoriously withhold the
identity of the immortalised friend. These circumstances hardly detract from
this poem's power, which itself confidently 'paces forth'.

But still sweet love is food for Fortunes tooth

Sweet love, renew thy force; be it not said
Thy edge should blunter be than appetite,
Which but to-day by feeding is allayed,
To-morrow sharp'ned in his former might.   4
So, love, be thou: although to-day thou fill
Thy hungry eyes even till they wink with fulness,
To-morrow see again, and do not kill
The spirit of love with a perpetual dulness.   8
Let this sad int'rim like the ocean be
Which parts the shore where two contracted new
Come daily to the banks, that, when they see
Return of love, more blest may be the view;   12
   Or call it winter, which, being full of care,
    Makes summer's welcome thrice more wished, more rare.

Sonnet 56   Quotation: *Troilus and Cressida* IV v 293

The ironic successor to 55's promise of immortality in verse: at the merely
human level, a call to love to renew itself. 'Wink with fulness' means 'fall asleep
after feeding'.

In love, i'faith, to the very tip of the nose

Being your slave, what should I do but tend
Upon the hours and times of your desire?
I have no precious time at all to spend,
Nor services to do till you require.   4
Nor dare I chide the world-without-end hour
Whilst I, my sovereign, watch the clock for you,
Nor think the bitterness of absence sour
When you have bid your servant once adieu.   8
Nor dare I question with my jealous thought
Where you may be, or your affairs suppose,
But, like a sad slave, stay and think of nought
Save where you are how happy you make those. 12
　　So true a fool is love that in your will,
　　Though you do anything, he thinks no ill.

Sonnet 57   Quotation: *Troilus and Cressida* III i 121

Despite the impassioned self-surrender the poem expresses, the effect of the
sonnet lies in part in the stealthy revision of 'your slave' into 'fool' (ll. 1 and 13).

What graces in my love do dwell
That he hath turn'd a heaven unto a hell

That god forbid that made me first your slave
I should in thought control your times of pleasure,
Or at your hand th' account of hours to crave,
Being your vassal bound to stay your leisure.   4
O, let me suffer, being at your beck,
Th' imprisoned absence of your liberty;
And patience, tame to sufferance, bide each check
Without accusing you of injury.   8
Be where you list; your charter is so strong
That you yourself may privilege your time
To what you will; to you it doth belong
Yourself to pardon of self-doing crime.   12
 I am to wait, though waiting so be hell,
 Not blame your pleasure, be it ill or well.

Sonnet 58   Quotation: *Midsummer Night's Dream* I i 206–7

Further self-humiliation, with the poet complaining in the form of saying he
has no right to complain, ostensibly making light of what he suffers, actually
being perfectly candid about it ('hell'). Line 6 is a multiple paradox. The
friend's 'liberty' (implying sexual licence) is a freedom which is an imprison-
ment; the poet suffering the absence of his over-free friend is also imprisoned.

Never durst poet touch a pen to write
Until his ink were temper'd with Love's sighs

If there be nothing new, but that which is
Hath been before, how are our brains beguiled,
Which, laboring for invention, bear amiss
The second burden of a former child!   4
O that record could with a backward look,
Even of five hundred courses of the sun,
Show me your image in some antique book,
Since mind at first in character was done: 8
That I might see what the old world could say
To this composèd wonder of your frame;
Whether we are mended, or whe'r better they,
Or whether revolution be the same   12
    O, sure I am the wits of former days
    To subjects worse have given admiring praise.

Sonnet 59   Quotation: *Love's Labour's Lost* IV iii 342–3

The self-reconciling sentiment ('It's all happened before') leads to the understatement ('I'm sure we improve on the past') with its rueful suggestion of the ironic 'I merely repeat the situation of praising a bad subject'. 'Character' (l.8) – writing; 'to this composed wonder of your frame' – 'in comparison with/ to equal your beauty', but also suggesting artistic rivalry with the past, the friend's beauty having prompted this composition.

Venus and Adonis: extracts

Venus and Adonis was written by Shakespeare in 1593, when the theatres were closed because of a severe outbreak of plague. Dedicated to the Earl of Southampton, it was Shakespeare's most popular success (9 editions in his lifetime, and often quoted, especially lines 229ff). The erotic-mythological narrative is based on Ovid, *Metamorphoses* X. Many poems in this genre (the 'epyllion') were written in the period.

Venus woos the frigid Adonis with all her eloquence and some physical force, learns with horror that he intends to hunt the boar, unavailingly dissuades him, and after he is gored fatally, passes her prophetic curse on love. He metamorphoses into a flower, while Venus leaves the earth.

Extract one: Venus begins her suit (lines 1–30)

> Even as the sun with purple-colored face
> Had ta'en his last leave of the weeping morn,
> Rose-cheeked Adonis hied him to the chase.
> Hunting he loved, but love he laughed to scorn.
>   Sick-thoughted Venus makes amain unto him
>   And like a bold-faced suitor 'gins to woo him.
>
> 'Thrice fairer than myself,' thus she began,
> 'The field's chief flower, sweet above compare,
> Stain to all nymphs, more lovely than a man,
> More white and red than doves or roses are,   10
>   Nature that made thee, with herself at strife,
>   Saith that the world hath ending with thy life.
>
> 'Vouchsafe, thou wonder, to alight thy steed,
> And rein his proud head to the saddlebow.
> If thou wilt deign this favor, for thy meed
> A thousand honey secrets shalt thou know.
>   Here come and sit, where never serpent hisses
>   And being set, I'll smother thee with kisses.

'And yet not cloy thy lips with loathed satiety,
But rather famish them amid their plenty,   20
Making them red and pale with fresh variety –
Ten kisses short as one, one long as twenty.
   A summer's day will seem an hour but short,
   Being wasted in such time-beguiling sport.'

With this she seizeth on his sweating palm,
The precedent of pith and livelihood,
And trembling in her passion, calls it balm,
Earth's sovereign salve to do a goddess good.
   Being so enraged, desire doth lend her force
   Courageously to pluck him from his horse.   30

Extract two: She argues that the time is right, describes her own
qualities, and puts the arguments for fruition (lines 115–74)

'Touch but my lips with those fair lips of thine –
Though mine be not so fair, yet are they red –
The kiss shall be thine own as well as mine.
What seest thou in the ground? Hold up thy head.
   Look in mine eyeballs, there thy beauty lies,
   Then why not lips on lips, since eyes in eyes?   120

'Art thou ashamed to kiss? Then wink again,
And I will wink – so shall the day seem night.
Love keeps his revels where there are but twain.
Be bold to play; our sport is not in sight.
   These blue-veined violets whereon we lean
   Never can blab, nor know not what we mean.

'The tender spring upon thy tempting lip
Shows thee unripe; yet mayst thou well be tasted.
Make use of time, let not advantage slip;
Beauty within itself should not be wasted.   130
   Fair flowers that are not gath'red in their prime
   Rot and consume themselves in little time.

'Were I hard-favored, foul, or wrinkled old,
Ill-nurtured, crooked, churlish, harsh in voice,
O'erworn, despisèd, rheumatic, and cold,
Thick-sighted, barren, lean and lacking juice
   Then mightst thou pause, for then I were not for thee;
   But having no defects, why dost abhor me?

'Thou canst not see one wrinkle in my brow;
Mine eyes are grey and bright and quick in turning;   140
My beauty as the spring doth yearly grow,
My flesh is soft and plump, my marrow burning;
   My smooth moist hand, were it with thy hand felt,
   Would in thy palm dissolve or seem to melt.

'Bid me discourse, I will enchant thine ear,
Or, like a fairy, trip upon the green,
Or, like a nymph, with long dishevelled hair,
Dance on the sands, and yet no footing seen.
   Love is a spirit all compact of fire,
   Not gross to sink, but light, and will aspire.   150

'Witness this primrose bank whereon I lie;
These forceless flowers like sturdy trees support me.
Two strengthless doves will draw me through the sky
From morn till night, even where I list to sport me.
   Is love so light, sweet boy, and may it be
   That thou should think it heavy unto thee?

'Is thine own heart to thine own face affected?
Can thy right hand seize love upon thy left?
Then woo thyself, be of thyself rejected;
Steal thine own freedom, and complain on theft.   160
   Narcissus so himself himself forsook.
   And died to kiss his shadow in the brook.

'Torches are made to light, jewels to wear,
Dainties to taste, fresh beauty for the use,
Herbs for their smell, and sappy plants to bear.
Things growing to themselves are growth's abuse.
    Seeds spring from seeds, and beauty breedeth beauty.
    Thou wast begot; to get it is thy duty.

'Upon the earth's increase why shouldst thou feed
Unless the earth with thy increase be fed?   170
By law of nature thou art bound to breed,
That thine may live when thou thyself art dead;
    And so, in spite of death, thou dost survive,
    In that thy likeness still is left alive.'

Extract three: She offers her body (lines 223–52)

Sometime she shakes her head, and then his hand;
Now gazeth she on him, now on the ground;
Sometime her arms infold him like a band –
She would, he will not in her arms be bound;
    And when from thence he struggles to be gone;
    She locks her lily fingers one in one.

'Fondling,' she saith, 'since I have hemmed thee here
Within the circuit of this ivory pale,   230
I'll be a park, and thou shalt be my deer:
Feed where thou wilt, on mountain or in dale;
    Graze on my lips; and if those hills be dry,
    Stray lower, where the pleasant fountains lie.

'Within this limit is relief enough,
Sweet bottom-grass, and high delightful plain,
Round rising hillocks, brakes obscure and rough,
To shelter thee from tempest and from rain.
    Then be my deer, since I am such a park;
    No dog shall rouse thee, though a thousand bark.' 240

At this Adonis smiles as in disdain,
That in each cheek appears a pretty dimple.
Love made those hollows, if himself were slain,
He might be buried in a tomb so simple,
   Foreknowing well, if there he came to lie,
   Why, there Love lived, and there he could not die.

These lovely caves, these round enchanting pits,
Opened their mouths to swallow Venus' liking.
Being mad before, how doth she now for wits?
Struck dead at first, what needs a second striking?   250
   Poor queen of love, in thine own law forlorn,
   To love a cheek that smiles at thee in scorn!

Extract four: She wins a kiss, and wrestles to take more (lines 535–76)

'Now let me say "Good night," and so say you.
If you will say so, you shall have a kiss.'
'Good night,' quoth she; and, ere he says 'Adieu,'
The honey fee of parting tend'red is:
   Her arms do lend his neck a sweet embrace;
   Incorporate then they seem; face grows to face;   540

Till breathless he disjoined, and backward drew
The heavenly moisture, that sweet coral mouth,
Whose precious taste her thirsty lips well knew,
Whereon they surfeit, yet complain on drouth.
   He with her plenty pressed, she faint with dearth,
   Their lips together glued, fall to the earth.

Now quick desire hath caught the yielding prey,
And glutton-like she feeds, yet never filleth.
Her lips are conquerors, his lips obey,
Paying what ransom the insulter willeth;   550
   Whose vulture thought doth pitch the price so high
   That she will draw his lips' rich treasure dry.

And having felt the sweetness of the spoil,
With blindfold fury she begins to forage.
Her face doth reek and smoke, her blood doth boil,
And careless lust stirs up a desperate courage,
　　Planting oblivion, beating reason back,
　　Forgetting shame's pure blush and honor's wrack.

Hot, faint, and weary with her hard embracing,
Like a wild bird being tamed with too much handling,　560
Or as the fleet-foot roe that's tired with chasing,
Or like the froward infant stilled with dandling,
　　He now obeys and now no more resisteth,
　　While she takes all she can, not all she listeth.

What wax so frozen but dissolves with temp'ring
And yields at last to every light impression?
Things out of hope are compassed oft with vent'ring,
Chiefly in love, whose leave exceeds commission,
　　Affection faints not like a pale-faced coward,
　　But then woos best when most his choice is froward.　570

When he did frown, O, had she then gave over,
Such nectar from his lips she had not sucked.
Foul words and frowns must not repel a lover.
What though the rose have prickles, yet 'tis plucked.
　　Were beauty under twenty locks kept fast,
　　Yet love breaks through and picks them all at last.

Extract five: Adonis counters that her 'love' is lust (lines 787–810)

'What have you urged that I cannot reprove?
The path is smooth that leadeth on to danger.
I hate not love, but your device in love,
That lends embracements unto every stranger.　　　　790
　　You do it for increase. O strange excuse,
　　When reason is the bawd to lust's abuse!

'Call it not love, for Love to heaven is fled
Since sweating Lust on earth usurped his name;
Under whose simple semblance he hath fed
Upon fresh beauty, blotting it with blame;
    Which the hot tyrant stains and soon bereaves,
    As caterpillars do the tender leaves.

'Love comforteth like sunshine after rain,   800
But Lust's effect is tempest after sun.
Love's gentle spring doth always fresh remain;
Lust's winter comes ere summer half be done.
    Love surfeits not, Lust like a glutton dies;
    Love is all truth, Lust full of forgèd lies.

'More I could tell, but more I dare not say:
The text is old, the orator too green.
Therefore in sadness now I will away.
My face is full of shame, my heart of teen;
    Mine ears, that to your wanton talk attended,
    Do burn themselves for having so offended.'   810

Extract six: Venus, after Adonis' death, prophesies that love will forever after be joined with sorrow (lines 1133–64)

    'Wonder of time,' quoth she, 'this is my spite,
      That, thou being dead, the day should yet be light.

'Since thou art dead, lo, here I prophesy
Sorrow on love hereafter shall attend.
It shall be waited on with jealousy,
Find sweet beginning, but unsavory end,
    Ne'er settled equally, but high or low,
    That all love's pleasure shall not match his woe.   1140

'It shall be fickle, false, and full of fraud,
Bud and be blasted in a breathing while,
The bottom poison, and the top o'erstrawed
With sweets that shall the truest sight beguile.
   The strongest body shall it make most weak,
   Strike the wise dumb, and teach the fool to speak.

'It shall be sparing, and too full of riot,
Teaching decrepit age to tread the measures;
The staring ruffian shall it keep in quiet,
Pluck down the rich, enrich the poor with treasures; 1150
   It shall be raging mad and silly mild,
   Make the young old, the old become a child.

'It shall suspect where is no cause of fear;
It shall not fear where it should most mistrust;
It shall be merciful, and too severe,
And most deceiving when it seems most just;
   Perverse it shall be where it shows most toward,
   Put fear to valor, courage to the coward.

'It shall be cause of war and dire events
And set dissension 'twixt the son and sire, 1160
Subject and servile to all discontents,
As dry combustious matter is to fire.
   Sith in his prime death doth my love destroy,
   They that love best their loves shall not enjoy.'

Extract one   l.3 'hied him' and l.5 'makes amain' – hastened; l.9 'stain' –
disgracing by surpassing; ll.11–12 ie, Nature exhausted herself to create him;
l.15 'meed' – reward; ll.25–6 'sweating palm' – see also ll.143–4. A sign of
sexual potential and erotic vigour. Elizabethan prostitutes would spit into their
palm to enhance their attractiveness to a potential client. Line 29 'enraged' –
aroused.

Extract two   l.121 'wink' – close your eyes; l.140 'grey' – used for blue eyes;
l.148 'footing' – footprint; l.151 – Venus, goddess of love, is at once aetherial
and physical; l.154 'list' – please; ll.163–74 – Shakespeare used substantially the
same topics in his first 17 sonnets, which urge on the young man his duty to
marry.

Extract three   l.229 'Fondling' – an endearment, literally 'foolish one';
hemm'd – enclosed; l.230 'pale' – a fence, made by her arms; 229ff – Venus
delightfully extends her pun on 'deer', thus 'relief' (l.235) means both
pasturage and sexual sport, 'bottom grass' (l.236) is grass growing in a valley,
and 'rouse' (l.240) is 'drive from cover' (dogs would, of course, be excluded from
a deer park).

Extract four   l.540 'incorporate' – grown into one; l.551 'vulture' – greedy;
ll.553–8 – the figure is military: she spoils and forages, 'oblivion' is planted like
a banner on a conquered place, reason having been driven back, she forgets all
other considerations; l.562 'froward' – contrary; l.564 'listeth' – wishes for;
l.568 – love takes a larger permission than has been granted.

Extract five   l.787 'reprove': has the senses of both 'rebuke' and 'refute'; l.797
'bereaves' – destroys; l.807 'in sadness' – in earnest; l.808 'teen' – has senses of
both 'anger' and 'grief'.

Extract six   l.1142 'breathing while' – a breath; l.1157 'toward' – docile; l.1163
'sith' – since.

A Poem for Shakespeare by Henry Willobie

Henry Willobie's publication *Willobie his Avisa* (1594) is one of the most famous of literary puzzles. It deals with the heroine, Avisa, fending off a series of suitors, the fifth of whom, 'H.W.', seems to be the author himself. He is rather maliciously encouraged by his 'familiar friend W.S. who not long before had tryed the curtesy of the like passion', who in the following poem is assuring H.W. of success 'because he would see whether an other could play his part better then himselfe, & in vewing far off the course of this loving Comedy, he determined to see whether it would sort to a happier end for this new actor, then it did for the old player'. Such histrionic metaphors were ubiquitous in this great age of drama, but there were some connections between Shakespeare and the author, via Shakespeare's friend Thomas Russell, and the work includes in one of its commendatory verses a direct allusion to Shakespeare as the author of *Lucrece*. There is some possibility, then, that this set of verses is voiced for Shakespeare, and has him giving robust advice on how to seduce, as the author's marginal comment disapprovingly notes. In l.29 'shoe' – 'show'.

W.S.

Well, say no more: I know thy griefe,
And face from whence these flames aryse,
It is not hard to fynd reliefe,
If thou wilt follow good advyse:
 She is no Saynt, She is no Nonne,
 I thinke in tyme she may be wonne.

At first repulse you must not faint,
Nor flye the field though she deny
You twise or thrise, yet manly bent,
Againe you must, and still reply: 10
 When tyme permits you not to talke,
 Then let your pen and fingers walke.

Apply her still with dyvers thinges,
(For giftes the wysest will deceave)
Sometymes with gold, sometymes with ringes,
No tyme nor fit occasion leave,
    Though coy at first she seeme and wielde,
    These toyes in tyme will make her yielde.

Looke what she likes; that you must love,
And what she hates, you must detest,   20
Where good or bad, you must approve,
The wordes and workes that please her best:
    If she be godly, you must sweare,
    That to offend you stand in feare.

You must commend her loving face,   Wicked wiles
For women joy in beauties praise,   to deceave
You must admire her sober grace,   witles women.
Her wisdome and her vertuous wayes,
    Say, t'was her wit & modest shoe,
    That made you like and love her so.   30

You must be secret, constant, free,
Your silent sighes & trickling teares,
Let her in secret often see,
Then wring her hand, as one that feares
    To speake, then wish she were your wife,
    And last desire her save your life.

When she doth laugh, you must be glad,
And watch occasions, tyme and place,
When she doth frowne, you must be sad,
Let sighes & sobbes request her grace: 40
    Sweare that your love is trulyment,
    So she in tyme must needes relent.

Twelfth Night: extracts and songs

Extract one

DUKE
    If music be the food of love, play on,
    Give me excess of it, that, surfeiting,
    The appetite may sicken, and so die.
    That strain again. It had a dying fall;
    O, it came o'er my ear like the sweet sound
    That breathes upon a bank of violets,
    Stealing and giving odor. Enough, no more.
    'Tis not so sweet now as it was before.
    O spirit of love, how quick and fresh art thou,
    That, notwithstanding thy capacity,   10
    Receiveth as the sea. Nought enters there,
    Of what validity and pitch soe'er,
    But falls into abatement and low price
    Even in a minute. So full of shapes is fancy
    That it alone is high fantastical.

Extract two

CLOWN   Would you have a love song, or a song of good life?
TOBY   A love song, a love song.
ANDREW   Ay, ay, I care not for good life.

          Clown sings.
    O mistress mine, where are you roaming?
    O, stay and hear! your true-love's coming,
        That can sing both high and low.
    Trip no further, pretty sweeting;
    Journeys end in lovers meeting,
        Every wise man's son doth know.

ANDREW   Excellent good, i' faith.
TOBY   Good, good.

Clown [sings].
What is love? 'Tis not hereafter;
Present mirth hath present laughter;
    What's to come is still unsure:
In delay there lies no plenty;
Then come kiss me, sweet and twenty,
    Youth's a stuff will not endure.

Extract three

Music plays
DUKE
Come hither, boy. If ever thou shalt love,
In the sweet pangs of it remember me;
For such as I am all true lovers are,
Unstaid and skittish in all motions else
Save in the constant image of the creature
That is beloved. How dost thou like this tune?   20
VIOLA
It gives a very echo to the seat
Where Love is throned.
DUKE   Thou dost speak masterly.
My life upon't, young though thou art, thine eye
Hath stayed upon some favor that it loves.
Hath it not, boy?
VIOLA   A little, by your favor.
DUKE
What kind of woman is't?
VIOLA   Of your complexion.
DUKE
She is not worth thee then. What years, i' faith?
VIOLA
About your years, my lord.

DUKE

    Too old, by heaven. Let still the woman take

    An elder than herself: so wears she to him,   30

    So sways she level in her husband's heart;

    For, boy, however we do praise ourselves,

    Our fancies are more giddy and unfirm,

    More longing, wavering, sooner lost and worn,

    Than women's are.

VIOLA   I think it well, my lord.

DUKE

    Then let thy love be younger than thyself,

    Or thy affection cannot hold the bent;

    For women are as roses, whose fair flow'r,

    Being once displayed, doth fall that very hour.

VIOLA

    And so they are; alas, that they are so.   40

    To die, even when they to perfection grow.

       Enter Curio and Clown.

DUKE

    O, fellow, come, the song we had last night.

    Mark it, Cesario; it is old and plain.

    The spinsters and the knitters in the sun,

    And the free maids that weave their thread with bones,

    Do use to chant it. It is silly sooth,

    And dallies with the innocence of love,

    Like the old age.

CLOWN   Are you ready, sir?

DUKE   I prithee sing.   50

       Music.

The Song.

Come away, come away, death,
    And in sad cypress let me be laid.
Fie away, fie away, breath;
    I am slain by a fair cruel maid.
My shroud of white, stuck all with yew,
      O, prepare it.
My part of death, no one so true
      Did share it.

Not a flower, not a flower sweet,
    On my black coffin let there be strown;   60
Not a friend, not a friend greet
    My poor corpse, where my bones shall be thrown.
A thousand thousand sighs to save,
      Lay me, O, where
Sad true lover never find my grave,
      To weep there.

Extract one　*Twelfth Night* (1601) I i 1–15. In this speech the love-stricken Orsino imagines (2–3) that music might allay the pangs of love, but discovers that the music, however exquisite, soon palls: anything else of whatsoever 'validity and pitch' (value and height) is diminished when it enters into the ever-receptive, swallowing sea of love. So despite the aspirations of music, love alone is 'high fantastical'.

Extract two　II iii 36–53. Feste sings to Sir Toby Belch and Sir Andrew Aguecheek a 'gather ye rosebuds while you may' love song. A 'song of good life' would have been a drinking song (Belch's main activity), Aguecheek misunderstands it as a moral song.

Extract three　II iv 15–66. Orsino and his boy 'Cesario' (Viola, who loves him, in disguise) talk about love while the tune for 'Come away, come away, death' is played, until Feste arrives to sing it. The expression 'hold the bent' is from archery: remain ready to shoot, ardent. 'Silly sooth' means 'simple truth', 'the old age' was the golden age of universal innocence. In the song, 'Come away' was idiomatic for 'come (along with me)', 'fie away' another idiom, 'begone for shame!'.

The Merchant of Venice: nocturne

Enter Lorenzo and Jessica.

LORENZO

The moon shines bright. In such a night as this,
When the sweet wind did gently kiss the trees
And they did make no noise, in such a night
Troilus methinks mounted the Troyan walls,
And sighed his soul toward the Grecian tents
Where Cressid lay that night.

JESSICA   In such a night
Did Thisbe fearfully o'ertrip the dew,
And saw the lion's shadow ere himself,
And ran dismayed away.

LORENZO   In such a night
Stood Dido with a willow in her hand   10
Upon the wild sea banks, and waft her love
To come again to Carthage.

JESSICA   In such a night
Medea gathered the enchanted herbs
That did renew old Aeson.

LORENZO   In such a night
Did Jessica steal from the wealthy Jew,
And with an unthrift love did run from Venice
As far as Belmont.

JESSICA   In such a night
Did young Lorenzo swear he loved her well,
Stealing her soul with many vows of faith,
And ne'er a true one.

LORENZO   In such a night   20
Did pretty Jessica, like a little shrew,
Slander her love, and he forgave it her.

JESSICA

I would out-night you, did nobody come;
But hark, I hear the footing of a man.

The Merchant of Venice (1596–7) V i 1–24. Lines 14–17 give the general context: Jessica is Shylock's daughter, now a Christian convert, and married to Lorenzo. The two refer to a series of famous and ill-fated lovers (though Aeson was the father of Medea's husband Jason), which either ironises them, or serves as an exorcism of disaster in love. Jessica's 'out-night you' joke means 'I could go on longer than you at this, but . . .'.

III

'THAT TIME OF YEAR THOU MAYST IN ME BEHOLD'

Sonnets predominantly on love and time; extracts with a commentary from *Antony and Cleopatra*; and three partings from the plays.

Sonnets

Like true, inseparable, faithful loves
Sticking together in calamity

Like as the waves make towards the pebbled shore,
So do our minutes hasten to their end;
Each changing place with that which goes before,
In sequent toil all forwards do contend.   4
Nativity, once in the main of light,
Crawls to maturity, wherewith being crowned,
Crooked eclipses 'gainst his glory fight,
And Time that gave doth now his gift confound.   8
Time doth transfix the flourish set on youth
And delves the parallels in beauty's brow,
Feeds on the rarities of nature's truth,
And nothing stands but for his scythe to mow: 12
    And yet to times in hope my verse shall stand,
    Praising thy worth, despite his cruel hand.

Sonnet 60   Quotation: *King John* III iv 66–7

60 is appropriate to its concern with minutes and hours. Line 5 – the new born child, as soon as it is in (or, which formerly was in) the 'main' (ocean/expanse) of light (etc). Eclipses (l.7) mean misfortune in astrology, with 'crook'd' suggesting age or disease. Line 9: Time's dart or arrow transfixes (pierces) the ornament set on youth.

since the substance of your perfect self
Is else devoted, I am but a shadow;
And to your shadow will I make true love

Is it thy will thy image should keep open
My heavy eyelids to the weary night?
Dost thou desire my slumbers should be broken
While shadows like to thee do mock my sight?   4
Is it thy spirit that thou send'st from thee
So far from home into my deeds to pry,
To find out shames and idle hours in me,
The scope and tenure of thy jealousy?   8
O no, thy love, though much, is not so great;
It is my love that keeps mine eye awake,
Mine own true love that doth my rest defeat
To play the watchman ever for thy sake.   12
    For thee watch I whilst thou dost wake elsewhere,
    From me far off, with others all too near.

Sonnet 61   Quotation: *Two Gentlemen* IV ii 119–21

Macbeth, Richard III and Brutus are among Shakespeare's insomniacs; the poet himself is here kept awake by the image of his friend, product of his love, for the friend is absent in spirit as well as in body: in 'thou dost wake elsewhere' (l.13), wake is 'revel' as much as 'not sleep'.

> *Love moderately; long love doth so;*
> *Too swift arrives as tardy as too slow*

Against my love shall be as I am now,
With Time's injurious hand crushed and o'erworn;
When hours have drained his blood and filled his brow
With lines and wrinkles, when his youthful morn   4
Hath travelled on to age's steepy night,
And all those beauties whereof now he's king
Are vanishing, or vanished out of sight,
Stealing away the treasure of his spring –   8
For such a time do I now fortify
Against confounding age's cruel knife,
That he shall never cut from memory
My sweet love's beauty, though my lover's life.   12
   His beauty shall in these black lines be seen,
   And they shall live, and he in them still green.

Sonnet 63   Quotation: *Romeo and Juliet* II vi 14–15

A triumphant complement to 49, the former poem's sense of personal
unworthiness transformed into the artist's triumph over time, and imagining
a future where the youth, rather than failing to acknowledge the poet (as 49),
has fallen prey to Time, from which only the poet's verse can rescue him.

On a love-book pray for my success . . .

When I have seen by Time's fell hand defaced
The rich proud cost of outworn buried age,
When sometime lofty towers I see down-rased
And brass eternal slave to mortal rage;   4
When I have seen the hungry ocean gain
Advantage on the kingdom of the shore,
And the firm soil win of the wat'ry main,
Increasing store with loss and loss with store;   8
When I have seen such interchange of state,
Or state itself confounded to decay,
Ruin hath taught me thus to ruminate,
That Time will come and take my love away.   12
  This thought is as a death, which cannot choose
  But weep to have that which it fears to lose.

Sonnet 64   Quotation: *Two Gentlemen* I i 19

Reflections upon mutability more melancholy in effect than 63: 'fell' (l.1) means 'deadly', 'weep to have' (l.14) both 'weep because it has what it "fears to lose"' and 'weep in desire to have'.

Love, love, nothing but love, still love, still more!

Since brass, nor stone, nor earth, nor boundless sea,
But sad mortality o'ersways their power,
How with this rage shall beauty hold a plea,
Whose action is no stronger than a flower?   4
O, how shall summer's honey breath hold out
Against the wrackful siege of batt'ring days,
When rocks impregnable are not so stout,
Nor gates of steel so strong but Time decays?   8
O fearful meditation: where, alack,
Shall Time's best jewel from Time's chest lie hid?
Or what strong hand can hold his swift foot back,
Or who his spoil of beauty can forbid?   12
     O, none, unless this miracle have might,
     That in black ink my love may still shine bright.

Sonnet 65   Quotation: *Troilus and Cressida* III i 108

Throughout this group of poems on Love and Time, 'my love' is shifting its sense away from 'my beloved' towards 'my loving'. Lines 3–4 are quoted memorably by Seamus Heaney in his essay on 'Belfast' (1972), in the context of the poet's helplessness in the face of political 'rage'.

The origin and commencement of his grief
Sprung from neglected love

Tired with all these, for restful death I cry:
As, to behold desert a beggar born,
And needy nothing trimmed in jollity,
And purest faith unhappily forsworn, 4
And gilded honor shamefully misplaced,
And maiden virtue rudely strumpeted,
And right perfection wrongfully disgraced,
And strength by limping sway disablèd, 8
And art made tongue-tied by authority,
And folly (doctor-like) controlling skill,
And simple truth miscalled simplicity,
And captive good attending captain ill. 12
    Tired with all these, from these would I be gone,
    Save that, to die, I leave my love alone.

Sonnet 66   Quotation: *Hamlet* III i 177–8

A dramatic example of the cumulative negation of twelve lines being set against the assertion made in the final couplet. W H Auden does a twentieth century version of the poem's allegory of wrongs in his 'August for the People' (1935). 'Desert' – person of merit; 'needy nothing' – a person devoid of substance; 'limping sway' – incompetent authority; 'controlling' – setting limits to.

Write loyal canzons of contemned love

No longer mourn for me when I am dead
Than you shall hear the surly sullen bell
Give warning to the world that I am fled
From this vile world, with vilest worms to dwell.   4
Nay, if you read this line, remember not
The hand that writ it, for I love you so
That I in your sweet thoughts would be forgot
If thinking on me then should make you woe.   8
O, if, I say, you look upon this verse
When I, perhaps, compounded am with clay,
Do not so much as my poor name rehearse,
But let your love even with my life decay,   12
    Lest the wise world should look into your moan
    And mock you with me after I am gone.

Sonnet 71   Quotation: *Twelfth Night* I v 254

Line 2 refers to the passing bell, tolled when a parishioner died. 'Warning' means 'notice', but also suggests the traditional 'remember you are to die' on a grave. Circulation of the sonnets in manuscript 'among his private friends' literalises ll.5–6. In l.11, note that the young man sonnets rarely play upon 'Will' in the way the Dark Lady sonnets do, which would have required the friend to repeat the poet's name (see 57 l.13, 89 l.7).

so eating love/Inhabits the finest wits of all

That time of year thou mayst in me behold
When yellow leaves, or none, or few, do hang
Upon those boughs which shake against the cold,
Bare ruined choirs where late the sweet birds sang.   4
In me thou seest the twilight of such day
As after sunset fadeth in the west,
Which by and by black night doth take away,
Death's second self that seals up all in rest.   8
In me thou seest the glowing of such fire
That on the ashes of his youth doth lie,
As the deathbed whereon it must expire,
Consumed with that which it was nourished by.   12
    This thou perceiv'st, which makes thy love more strong,
    To love that well which thou must leave ere long.

Sonnet 73   Quotation: *Two Gentlemen* I i 43–4

The metaphoric language of this imaginatively resonant sonnet has received much attention: to some the winter trees of ll.2–4 suggest ruined monasteries, the original spelling of 'choirs' as 'quiers' has been seen with 'yellow leaves' as suggesting faded or outmoded poetry. In the context of human transience so established, 'love that well' in l.14 could be 'your youth' as well as 'me'.

Love is a smoke raised with the fume of sighs

But be contented: when that fell arrest
Without all bail shall carry me away,
My life hath in this line some interest
Which for memorial still with thee shall stay.   4
When thou reviewest this, thou dost review
The very part was consecrate to thee:
The earth can have but earth, which is his due;
My spirit is thine, the better part of me.   8
So then thou hast but lost the dregs of life,
The prey of worms, my body being dead,
The coward conquest of a wretch's knife,
Too base of thee to be rememberèd.   12
    The worth of that is that which it contains,
    And that is this, and this with thee remains.

Sonnet 74   Quotation: *Romeo and Juliet* I i 188

The sonnet continues the main sense of 73 ll.13–14. 'Fell' means 'deadly';
'review' (l.5), 'look again at'; l.7 echoes the burial service. In l.13, the first 'that'
is the body, the second the spirit, which in l.14 is equated with the poetry which
will remain after the poet's bodily death.

Love's tongue proves dainty Bacchus gross in taste

So are you to my thoughts as food to life,
Or as sweet-seasoned showers are to the ground;
And for the peace of you I hold such strife
As 'twixt a miser and his wealth is found: 4
Now proud as an enjoyer, and anon
Doubting the filching age will steal his treasure;
Now counting best to be with you alone,
Then bettered that the world may see my pleasure; 8
Sometime all full with feasting on your sight,
And by and by clean starvèd for a look,
Possessing or pursuing no delight
Save what is had or must from you be took.   12
    Thus do I pine and surfeit day by day,
    Or gluttoning on all, or all away.

Sonnet 75   Quotation: *Love's Labour's Lost* IV iii 335

The sonnet explores in ways which are, for Shakespeare, quite conventional, the paradoxical existence of the lover, simultaneously uplifted and cast down by the same experience. The simile of the miser and of the 'filching age' recalls 48 and 52, 'doubting' (l.6) is 'fearing'; 'clean' (l.10) 'wholly'; 'Or . . . or' was used for 'Either . . . or', 'all away' means 'lacking everything' (l.14).

For thee I'll lock up all the gates of love

Farewell: thou art too dear for my possessing,
And like enough thou know'st thy estimate.
The charter of thy worth gives thee releasing;
My bonds in thee are all determinate.   4
For how do I hold thee but by thy granting,
And for that riches where is my deserving?
The cause of this fair gift in me is wanting,
And so my patent back again is swerving.   8
Thyself thou gav'st, thy own worth then not knowing,
Or me, to whom thou gav'st it, else mistaking;
So thy great gift, upon misprision growing,
Comes home again, on better judgment making.   12
    Thus have I had thee as a dream doth flatter,
    In sleep a king, but waking no such matter.

Sonnet 87   Quotation: *Much Ado* IV i 104

The sonnet develops 'dear' (precious/costly) in the opening line into an extended financial-legal metaphor: 1.2 'estimate' – value; 1.3 'charter' – privilege (cf. the youth's social rank); 1.4 'bonds in' – claim upon you; 'determinate' – expired; 1.8 'back again is swerving' – returns to you; 1.11 'misprision' – a mistake. The final couplet suggests both the vanished dream of possession in which the poet was a king, and also a dream in which the youth was a king, but on waking ... (etc).

love may transform me to an oyster . . .

When thou shalt be disposed to set me light
And place my merit in the eye of scorn,
Upon thy side against myself I'll fight
And prove thee virtuous, though thou art forsworn. 4
With mine own weakness being best acquainted,
Upon thy part I can set down a story
Of faults concealed wherein I am attainted,
That thou, in losing me, shall win much glory: 8
And I by this will be a gainer too;
For, bending all my loving thoughts on thee,
The injuries that to myself I do,
Doing thee vantage, double-vantage me. 12
   Such is my love, to thee I so belong,
   That for thy right myself will bear all wrong.

Sonnet 88   Quotation: *Much Ado* II iii 25

Develops ll.6–7 of 87, the poet ostensibly offering to justify the young man by
confessing to his own concealed faults. But ll.5–7 could also suggest 'your faults
which have tainted me'; 'bear' in l.14 hints at 'lay bare' as well as 'take the
burden of'.

This is the very ecstasy of love
Whose violent property fordoes itself

Say that thou didst forsake me for some fault,
And I will comment upon that offence;
Speak of my lameness, and I straight will halt,
Against thy reasons making no defence.   4
Thou canst not, love, disgrace me half so ill,
To set a form upon desirèd change,
As I'll myself disgrace; knowing thy will,
I will acquaintance strangle and look strange,   8
Be absent from thy walks, and in my tongue
Thy sweet belovèd name no more shall dwell,
Lest I, too much profane, should do it wrong
And haply of our old acquaintance tell.   12
    For thee, against myself I'll vow debate,
    For I must ne'er love him whom thou dost hate.

Sonnet 89   Quotation: *Hamlet* II i 102–3

In 89, the talk of 'faults concealed' in 88 develops into preposterous inventions
of self-disgracing ('speak of my lameness and I straight will halt', ie. limp) to
substantiate reasons for the youth's desertion. There is a quibble between 'set
a form' and 'dis-grace', l.7 allows the latent will/Will pun to appear.

The course of true love never did run smooth

Then hate me when thou wilt; if ever, now;
Now, while the world is bent my deeds to cross,
Join with the spite of fortune, make me bow,
And do not drop in for an after-loss. 4
Ah, do not, when my heart hath scaped this sorrow,
Come in the rearward of a conquered woe;
Give not a windy night a rainy morrow,
To linger out a purposed overthrow. 8
If thou wilt leave me, do not leave me last,
When other petty griefs have done their spite,
But in the onset come: so shall I taste
At first the very worst of fortune's might; 12
    And other strains of woe, which now seem woe,
    Compared with loss of thee will not seem so.

Sonnet 90   Quotation: *Midsummer Night's Dream* I i 134

'Hate' in l.1 takes up the last word of 89; lines 1–2 'now/Now' – now is actually a rare word in the sequence (here and 100 l.9 only), which gives this rightly praised poem a particular aspect of crisis.

Then loving goes by haps
Some Cupid kills with arrows, some with traps

So shall I live, supposing thou art true,
Like a deceivèd husband; so love's face
May still seem love to me though altered new,
Thy looks with me, thy heart in other place.   4
For there can live no hatred in thine eye;
Therefore in that I cannot know thy change;
In many's looks the false heart's history
Is writ in moods and frowns and wrinkles strange: 8
But heaven in thy creation did decree
That in thy face sweet love should ever dwell;
Whate'er thy thoughts or thy heart's workings be,
Thy looks should nothing thence but sweetness tell. 12
    How like Eve's apple doth thy beauty grow
    If thy sweet virtue answer not thy show!

Sonnet 93   Quotation: *Much Ado* III i 105–6

See Introduction for George Eliot's use of this sonnet, which takes up the idea of being hated by the young man from 90. 'There's no art to find the mind's construction in the face', mused Duncan in *Macbeth*; 'many's' (l.7) – of many people.

Loves him with that excellence
That angels love good men with

They that have pow'r to hurt and will do none,
That do not do the thing they most do show,
Who, moving others, are themselves as stone,
Unmovèd, cold, and to temptation slow;   4
They rightly do inherit heaven's graces
And husband nature's riches from expense;
They are the lords and owners of their faces,
Others but stewards of their excellence.   8
The summer's flow'r is to the summer sweet,
Though to itself it only live and die;
But if that flow'r with base infection meet,
The basest weed outbraves his dignity: 12
    For sweetest things turn sourest by their deeds;
    Lilies that fester smell far worse than weeds.

Sonnet 94   Quotation: *Henry VIII* II ii 31–2

This famous sonnet, a Mona Lisa in poetry, in part continues the thought of 93, having an enigma as its subject. The poem proceeds by making the type of person described alternately attractive and, faintly, repellent. There is no mention of the poet or his beloved. Shakespeare apparently distrusted stoicity and the self-repressed. The sestet here (9–14) repeats a basic tragic perception in Shakespeare, that the corruption of the best is the worst.

> *But I love thee*
> *By love's own sweet constraint*

How sweet and lovely dost thou make the shame
Which, like a canker in the fragrant rose,
Doth spot the beauty of thy budding name!
O, in what sweets dost thou thy sins enclose!   4
That tongue that tells the story of thy days,
Making lascivious comments on thy sport,
Cannot dispraise but in a kind of praise;
Naming thy name blesses an ill report.   8
O, what a mansion have those vices got
Which for their habitation chose out thee,
Where beauty's veil doth cover every blot
And all things turns to fair that eyes can see!   12
    Take heed, dear heart, of this large privilege;
    The hardest knife ill used doth lose his edge.

Sonnet 95   Quotation: *All's Well* IV ii 15–16

The outspoken censure here is partly the product of the moral authority won
in 94. The residual vocabulary of a normal sonnet – 'fragrant rose', 'mansion',
'beauty's veil' (etc) enacts 'dispraise but in a kind of praise' before the brutal
phallic proverb of l.14. The concern with 'name' is most prominent here of all
the sonnets. It reminds the friend of the honour he is losing to 'shame' and
gossip.

Love's thrice-repured nectar

How like a winter hath my absence been
From thee, the pleasure of the fleeting year!
What freezings have I felt, what dark days seen,
What old December's bareness everywhere!   4
And yet this time removed was summer's time,
The teeming autumn, big with rich increase,
Bearing the wanton burden of the prime,
Like widowed wombs after their lords' decease: 8
Yet this abundant issue seemed to me
But hope of orphans and unfathered fruit;
For summer and his pleasures wait on thee,
And, thou away, the very birds are mute;   12
   Or, if they sing, 'tis with so dull a cheer
   That leaves look pale, dreading the winter's near.

Sonnet 97   Quotation: *Troilus and Cressida* III ii 21

To assign to the beloved a power greater than Nature's was a normal gambit
for Renaissance love poetry: absence from the friend disorders the seasons for
the poet, making summer into December, the autumn into a time of
bereavement rather than fruition, because the 'abundant issue' finds itself
orphaned by the friend's absence. 'Prime' (l.7) – spring.

He seems to have the quotidian of love upon him

From you have I been absent in the spring,
When proud-pied April, dressed in all his trim,
Hath put a spirit of youth in everything,
That heavy Saturn laughed and leapt with him;   4
Yet nor the lays of birds, nor the sweet smell
Of different flowers in odor and in hue,
Could make me any summer's story tell,
Or from their proud lap pluck them where they grew: 8
Nor did I wonder at the lily's white,
Nor praise the deep vermilion in the rose;
They were but sweet, but figures of delight,
Drawn after you, you pattern of all those.   12
    Yet seemed it winter still, and you away,
    As with your shadow I with these did play.

Sonnet 98   Quotation: *As You Like It* III ii 339

'Saturn' (l.4) was associated with melancholy; l.5 'lays' – songs; l.7 'make me
any summer's story tell' ie. a story of love, pleasure, merriment, cp. 'a sad tale's
best for winter' (*Winter's Tale* II i 25).

Antony and Cleopatra: The Mutual Twain

Cleopatra's suicide has just outmanoeuvred the Romans:

> 'Is that well done, Charmian? Verie well sayd she againe,
> & meete for a Princes[s] discended from the race of so
> many noble kings. She sayd no more, but fell down dead
> hard by the bed.'
>
> (Plutarch trans. Lord North, 1579)

If you look at a text of the play, you will see that Shakespeare versified this passage very directly (V ii 325–6). But 'she sayd no more' didn't suit his instincts, and he gave Charmian two more words which add to her 'life' even at this final moment: 'Ah, soldier!'.

Dying groans in Shakespeare are commonly 'O' sounds: these last words of Charmian are a sigh, her farewell to life, expressing regret for what can be had no more, which the soldier represents: he is in this brief moment not a Roman adversary to be exulted over, but a man, addressed by a woman whose life has been given over to ease and pleasure. Tragic nobility in death is one thing, but something needed to be added to express what it means to say farewell to such a life.

Antony and Cleopatra, Shakespeare's great love-tragedy, has often struck critics as (in essence) having too much of 'Ah, soldier!' about it, too great a feeling for dalliance; while the deuteragonists seem irresponsible, wasteful, frivolous. Antony acquires, we are told by such moralists, no tragic knowledge in his fall. Two empires are lost, Antony's half of the Roman world, and Cleopatra's Egyptian empire, and 'all for love'. He can say, and seriously mean, that Cleopatra's bosom was his coronet, 'my chief end' (IV xii 27), but Cleopatra is hardly like Juliet, in her lack of alacrity to share her lover's fate.

Shakespeare turned to the subject at the height of his dramatic and poetic powers. He would have been about 44. In the source, Plutarch, Antony's love for Cleopatra is depicted as 'the last and extreamest mischiefe of all other' to have befallen him, and so throughout the play there appear those willing to 'Name Cleopatra as she is call'd in Rome', even Antony himself at moments of anger. But Shakespeare kept from Antony the one speech that would have settled our responses and locked them into the adverse view of the lovers taken by those moralistic critics: Antony never has a soliloquy of regret, asking himself why he has sacrificed so much for this woman. There was a more subtle effect too: Mark Antony does not participate in bawdy talk. He expresses his love as love, no gross sexual reference or jesting allows us to find condemnation in his own words. He remains a noble Roman in his love: 'No more light answers' (I ii 174), he reproves the quibbling Enobarbus.

Shakespeare did not seek to disguise the fact that these are two middle aged lovers (they were 43 and 29 when they met, ten years older at their deaths), but the children they had are only mentioned in the text. The love between Antony and Cleopatra is unstable. It switches between mutual re-inforcement and doing, as far as the relationship's continuance is concerned, the worst thing possible: Antony marries Octavia, Cleopatra deserts him at Actium.

The physical passion of the two is not, like that of Romeo and Juliet, made delicate by being the first discovery of such feelings. The continuous sexual reference in what Cleopatra says expresses fully what they mean to one another. But Shakespeare does not leave them alone together. He was writing for a boy player (of Cleopatra), and had recourse to one of his habitual facilitating devices: as in the comedies of love, Cleopatra captivates by being contrary. He radically altered the arts of Plutarch's 'Queene of all flatterers', who 'every way framed her countenance, that when Antonius came to see her, she cast her eyes upon him, like a woman ravished for joy. Straight againe when he went from her, she fell a weeping and blubbering, looked rufully of the matter, and stil found the meanes that Antonius should oftentymes finds her weeping'. Cleopatra is an Egyptian Rosalind, 'the wiser, the waywarder': it is love with a lot of friction in it:

CLEOPATRA
  Where is he?
CHARMIAN   I did not see him since.
CLEOPATRA
  See where he is, who's with him, what he does:
  I did not send you. If you find him sad,
  Say I am dancing; if in mirth, report
  That I am sudden sick. Quick, and return. *[Exit Alexas.]*
CHARMIAN
  Madam, methinks, if you did love him dearly,
  You do not hold the method to enforce
  The like from him.
CLEOPATRA   What should I do, I do not?
CHARMIAN
  In each thing give him way, cross him in nothing.
CLEOPATRA
  Thou teachest like a fool: the way to lose him!

(I iii 1–10)

'She is cunning past man's thought' says Antony (I ii 143): and beyond woman's too, as we see in Charmian's incomprehension.

  Cleopatra's deep appreciation of her erotic self extends to moods of self-congratulation in which she makes herself sound like a professional:

>   Give me some music; music, moody food
>   Of us that trade in love.

(II v 1–2)

Nor does she confine her reveries to the present lover, though he offers the promise of power which most satisfies her:

CLEOPATRA
    Thou, eunuch Mardian!
MARDIAN   What's your Highness' pleasure?
CLEOPATRA
    Not now to hear thee sing. I take no pleasure
    In aught an eunuch has: 'tis well for thee
    That, being unseminared, thy freer thoughts
    May not fly forth of Egypt. Has thou affections?
MARDIAN   Yes, gracious madam.
CLEOPATRA   Indeed?
MARDIAN
    Not in deed, madam; for I can do nothing
    But what indeed is honest to be done:
    Yet have I fierce affections, and think
    What Venus did with Mars.
CLEOPATRA   O Charmian,
    Where think'st thou he is now? Stands he, or sits he?
    Or does he walk? or is he on his horse?
    O happy horse, to bear the weight of Antony!
    Do bravely, horse! for wot'st thou whom thou mov'st?
    The demi-Atlas of this earth, the arm
    And burgonet of men. He's speaking now,
    Or murmuring, 'Where's my serpent of old Nile?'
    (For so he calls me). Now I feed myself
    With most delicious poison. Think on me,
    That am with Phoebus' amorous pinches black
    And wrinkled deep in time! Broad-fronted Caesar,
    When thou wast here above the ground, I was
    A morsel for a monarch; and great Pompey
    Would stand and make his eyes grow in my brow;
    There would he anchor his aspect, and die
    With looking on his life.
        Enter Alexas.
ALEXAS   Sovereign of Egypt, hail!
CLEOPATRA
    How much unlike art thou Mark Antony!
    Yet, coming from him, that great med'cine hath

With his tinct gilded thee.
How goes it with my brave Mark Antony?

ALEXAS

Last thing he did, dear Queen,
He kissed – the last of many doubled kisses –
This orient pearl. His speech sticks in my heart.

CLEOPATRA

Mine ear must pluck it thence.

ALEXAS   'Good friend,' quoth he,
'Say the firm Roman to great Egypt sends
This treasure of an oyster; at whose foot,
To mend the petty present, I will piece
Her opulent throne with kingdoms.

(I v 8–47)

That power can manifest itself in her casual cruelties:

That Herod's head
I'll have: but how, when Antony is gone,
Through whom I might command it?

(III iii 4–6)

Her most brilliant eloquence in love is always sharpened by an element
of calculation:

ANTONY   Most sweet queen –

CLEOPATRA

Nay, pray you seek no colour for your going,
But bid farewell, and go: when you sued staying,
Then was the time for words: no going then,
Eternity was in our lips and eyes,
Bliss in our brows' bent: none our parts so poor
But was a race of heaven.

(I iii 31–7)

– wonderful, but she is being deliberately provoking to Antony. Her great 'dream of Antony speech' in Act V simultaneously apotheosises the dead Antony, and recruits the sympathies of Dolabella, from whom she must elicit the intentions of Caesar. He tries to interrupt her, to resist, but collapses and blabs immediately after this:

DOLABELLA
  Most noble Empress, you have heard of me?
CLEOPATRA
  I cannot tell.
DOLABELLA   Assuredly you know me.
CLEOPATRA
  No matter, sir, what I have heard or known.
  You laugh when boys or women tell their dreams;
  Is't not your trick?
DOLABELLA   I understand not, madam.
CLEOPATRA
  I dreamt there was an Emperor Antony.
  O, such another sleep, that I might see
  But such another man.
DOLABELLA   If it might please ye –
CLEOPATRA
  His face was as the heav'ns, and therein stuck
  A sun and moon, which kept their course and lighted
  The little O, th' earth.
DOLABELLA   Most sovereign creature –
CLEOPATRA
  His legs bestrid the ocean: his reared arm
  Crested the world: his voice was propertied
  As all the tunèd spheres, and that to friends;
  But when he meant to quail and shake the orb,
  He was as rattling thunder. For his bounty,
  There was no winter in't: an autumn 'twas
  That grew the more by reaping: his delights
  Were dolphin-like, they showed his back above

> The element they lived in: in his livery
> Walked crowns and crownets: realms and islands were
> As plates dropped from his pocket.
>
> DOLABELLA   Cleopatra –
>
> CLEOPATRA
> Think you there was or might be such a man
> As this I dreamt of?
>
> DOLABELLA   Gentle madam, no.
>
> CLEOPATRA
> You lie, up to the hearing of the gods.
> But if there be nor ever were one such,
> It's past the size of dreaming: nature wants stuff
> To vie strange forms with fancy, yet t' imagine
> An Antony were nature's piece 'gainst fancy,
> Condemning shadows quite.

(V ii 71–100)

Antony's love is expressed in hyperboles. He is given the conceits of a sonneteer. His parting words to Cleopatra, ending the first movement of the play:

> Let us go. Come;
> Our separation so abides and flies,
> That thou, residing here, goes yet with me;
> And I, hence fleeting, here remain with thee.

(I iii 101–4)

take us back to the lyric mood of his opening words:

> ANTONY
> Let Rome in Tiber melt and the wide arch
> Of the ranged empire fall! Here is my space,
> Kingdoms are clay: our dungy earth alike
> Feeds beast as man. The nobleness of life

Is to do thus; when such a mutual pair
And such a twain can do't, in which I bind,
On pain of punishment, the world to weet
We stand up peerless.

CLEOPATRA   Excellent falsehood!
Why did he marry Fulvia, and not love her?
I'll seem the fool I am not. Antony
Will be himself.

ANTONY   But stirred by Cleopatra.
Now for the love of Love and her soft hours,
Let's not confound the time with conference harsh.
There's not a minute of our lives should stretch
Without some pleasure now. What sport to-night?

CLEOPATRA

Hear the ambassadors.

ANTONY   Fie, wrangling queen!
Whom every thing becomes – to chide, to laugh,
To weep; whose every passion fully strives
To make itself, in thee, fair and admired.
No messenger but thine, and all alone
To-night we'll wander through the streets and note
The qualities of people. Come, my queen;
Last night you did desire it. – Speak not to us.
          Exeunt [Antony and Cleopatra] with the Train.

(I i 33–55)

Katherine Mansfield considered the last four lines of the passage 'so *true* a pleasure of lovers', the parting words of Antony in I iii 'beautiful lines' (*The Critical Writings of Katherine Mansfield* ed Clare Hanson (Macmillan, 1987) p.121).

Notice that 'On pain of punishment': their love is in part based on what they can do to other people, if they choose to do so: heady, naked and cruel exertions of power. We have seen it in Cleopatra ('that Herod's head/I'll have'). Erotic cruelty haunts the play ('Phoebus' amorous pinches' . . . 'The stroke of death is as a lover's pinch/Which hurts, and is desir'd' . . . 'made/The water which they beat to follow

faster,/ As amorous of their strokes' . . . 'I'll make death love me' (I v 28;
V ii 294–5; II ii 195–7; III xiii 193).

It is therefore appropriate that they are at their height, their best
unanimity, when Antony returns from victory in battle:

> *Enter Cleopatra*
> ANTONY *[To Scarus]*   Give me thy hand;
>   To this great fairy I'll commend thy acts,
>   Make her thanks bless thee. – O thou day o' th' world,
>   Chain mine armed neck; leap thou, attire and all,
>   Through proof of harness to my heart, and there
>   Ride on the pants triumphing.
> CLEOPATRA   Lord of lords!
>   O infinite virtue, com'st thou smiling from
>   The world's great snare uncaught?
> ANTONY   My nightingale,
>   We have beat them to their beds. What, girl! though grey
>   Do something mingle with our younger brown, yet ha' we
>   A brain that nourishes our nerves, and can
>   Get goal for goal of youth. Behold this man:
>   Commend unto his lips thy favouring hand. –
>   Kiss it, my warrior. – He hath fought to-day
>   As if a god in hate of mankind had
>   Destroyed in such a shape.
> CLEOPATRA   I'll give thee, friend,
>   An armor all of gold; it was a king's.
> ANTONY
>   He has deserved it, were it carbuncled
>   Like holy Phoebus' car.

(IV viii 11–29)

Notice here his continuously varied naming of her. Antony's names
for Cleopatra are a love-poem in themselves: Thetis, great Egypt,
sweet, charm, enchanting queen, my serpent of old Nile, and (here) day
o' the world, great fairy, nightingale. There are his insults too: thou
spell, witch, right gypsy, a boggler.

The play depicts Antony throughout as engaged in prodigious giving
– often to subordinates, but mainly to Cleopatra, a literal, political,
sexual, and onomastic prodigality. Opponents and allies are left to
commentate with dismay: he 'gives his potent regiment to a trull'
(III vi 95), 'we have kiss'd away kingdoms' (III x 6). As astonishing is
the rapidity of his forgiveness of her:

> Fall not a tear, I say, one of them rates
> All that is won and lost: give me a kiss,
> Even this repays me

> (III xi 69–71)

Enobarbus perceives what is happening as an emptying-out of Antony
('that he should dream . . . the full Caesar will/Answer his emptiness'
III xiii 34–7). It seems that, in performance, at the Globe or in the
Blackfriars indoor theatre, there was one final startling stage effect,
making graphic this emptying of a man who has given kingdoms,
treasures, 'potent regiment', forgiveness. As Burbage, playing Antony,
was hoisted up into Cleopatra's monument, his blood splattered down
on his guard. (The poet Samuel Daniel saw this, and incorporated the
vivid detail into a revision of his own Cleopatra play.) Antony dies
when he has lived, kissing Cleopatra once more; and when there is
nowhere else for her to turn, Cleopatra dies imagining re-union with
him, revisiting in her imagination her triumph of seduction, looking:

> As she would catch another Antony
> In her strong toil of grace

> (V ii 345–6)

Despite the moralising of disapproving critics, what else could Antony
have done but give all for love? For:

Age cannot wither her, nor custom stale
Her infinite variety: other women cloy
The appetites they feed, but she makes hungry
Where most she satisfies. For vilest things
Become themselves in her, that the holy priests
Bless her when she is riggish.

(II ii 234–9)

– Ah, soldier!

Separations: play extracts

Extract one: Richard II

QUEEN
And must we be divided? Must we part?
RICHARD
Ay, hand from hand, my love, and heart from heart.
QUEEN
Banish us both, and send the king with me.
NORTHUMBERLAND
That were some love, but little policy.
QUEEN
Then whither he goes, thither let me go.
RICHARD
So two, together weeping, make one woe.
Weep thou for me in France, I for thee here.
Better far off than near, be ne'er the near.
Go, count thy way with sighs; I mine with groans.
QUEEN
So longest way shall have the longest moans.   90
RICHARD
Twice for one step I'll groan, the way being short,
And piece the way out with a heavy heart.
Come, come, in wooing sorrow let's be brief,
Since, wedding it, there is such length in grief.
One kiss shall stop our mouths, and dumbly part.
Thus give I mine, and thus take I thy heart.
QUEEN
Give me mine own again. 'Twere no good part
To take on me to keep and kill thy heart.
So, now I have mine own again, be gone,
That I may strive to kill it with a groan.   100

RICHARD
 We make woe wanton with this fond delay.
 Once more adieu! The rest let sorrow say.   *Exeunt.*

Extract two: Troilus and Cressida

TROILUS
 Dear, trouble not yourself; the morn is cold.
CRESSIDA
 Then, sweet my lord, I'll call mine uncle down;
 He shall unbolt the gates.
TROILUS   Trouble him not;
 To bed, to bed. Sleep kill those pretty eyes,
 And give as soft attachment to thy senses
 As infants' empty of all thought!
CRESSIDA   Good morrow then.
TROILUS
 I prithee now, to bed.
CRESSIDA   Are you aweary of me?
TROILUS
 O Cressida, but that the busy day,
 Waked by the lark, hath roused the ribald crows,
 And dreaming night will hide our joys no longer,   10
 I would not from thee.
CRESSIDA   Night hath been too brief.
TROILUS
 Beshrew the witch! with venomous wights she stays
 As tediously as hell, but flies the grasps of love
 With wings more momentary-swift than thought.
 You will catch cold and curse me.
CRESSIDA   Prithee, tarry;
 You men will never tarry.
 O foolish Cressid! I might have still held off,
 And then you would have tarried. Hark, there's one up.

Extract three: Cymbeline

IMOGEN   What was the last
　That he spake to thee?
PISANIO   It was his queen, his queen.
IMOGEN
　Then waved his handkerchief?
PISANIO   And kissed it, madam.
IMOGEN
　Senseless linen, happier therein than I!
　And that was all?
PISANIO   No, madam. For so long
　As he could make me with this eye or ear
　Distinguish him from others, he did keep   10
　The deck, with glove or hat or handkerchief
　Still waving, as the fits and stirs of's mind
　Could best express how slow his soul sailed on,
　How swift his ship.
IMOGEN   Thou shouldst have made him
　As little as a crow or less, ere left
　To after-eye him.
PISANIO   Madam, so I did.
IMOGEN
　I would have broke mine eyestrings, cracked them but
　To look upon him till the diminution
　Of space had pointed him sharp as my needle;
　Nay, followed him till he had melted from   20
　The smallness of a gnat to air, and then
　Have turned mine eye and wept.

Extract one *Richard II* (1595) V i 81–102. Richard has been deposed, and here says farewell to his Queen. Northumberland sides with Henry IV, the new King; Richard's guards and the queen's attendants are also present. They speak while kissing three times, and use the conceit in which a kiss exchanges hearts. In l.88 'ne'er the near' (ie. 'nearer') means 'not together'; 'wanton' in l.101 is 'unrestrained', but also refers to the sexual element in their kissing.

Extract two *Troilus and Cressida* (1602) IV ii 1–18. Line 4 'kill' – overpower; l.5 'attachment' – imprisonment; l.12 'with venomous wights she stays' – Shakespeare thinks of his insomniac assassins, Brutus, Macbeth, Richard III.

Extract three *Cymbeline* (1610) I iii 4–22. Imogen, a princess, quizzes Pisanio, servant of her husband, about how her husband (Posthumus Leonatus) departed into banishment.

IV

'WINTERS COLD'

Sonnets dealing with the poet's own betrayal of his love; extracts from Lucrece, *and the sonnets to the 'Dark Lady' (though these sonnets never call her a Lady, and 'dark' only once!).*

The volume ends with a vision of perfect love departed from the earth, *The Phoenix and Turtle*, and extracts from Shakespeare's last surviving work, *The Two Noble Kinsmen*, on friendship and the frightening power of Love.

Sonnets

imperial Love, that God most high

To me, fair friend, you never can be old,
For as you were when first your eye I eyed,
Such seems your beauty still. Three winters cold
Have from the forests shook three summers' pride, 4
Three beauteous springs to yellow autumn turned
In process of the seasons have I seen,
Three April perfumes in three hot Junes burned,
Since first I saw you fresh, which yet are green. 8
Ah, yet doth beauty, like a dial hand,
Steal from his figure, and no pace perceived;
So your sweet hue, which methinks still doth stand,
Hath motion, and mine eye may be deceived; 12
    For fear of which, hear this, thou age unbred:
    Ere you were born was beauty's summer dead.

Sonnet 104   Quotation: *All's Well* II iii 73

The affirmations of this sonnet become uncertainties; its considerable effect is won from melancholy self-contradiction – 'you never can be old' versus the last line, which might be read to imply that even the poet saw his friend's beauty had passed. 'Figure' (l.10) is a complex word: the numerical figure on a watch face, the bodily beauty of the friend, and beauty departing from its own height of excellence.

I'll have them very fairly bound: All books of love

When in the chronicle of wasted time
I see descriptions of the fairest wights,
And beauty making beautiful old rime
In praise of ladies dead and lovely knights;   4
Then, in the blazon of sweet beauty's best,
Of hand, of foot, of lip, of eye, of brow,
I see their antique pen would have expressed
Even such a beauty as you master now.   8
So all their praises are but prophecies
Of this our time, all you prefiguring;
And, for they looked but with divining eyes,
They had not skill enough your worth to sing: 12
    For we, which now behold these present days,
    Have eyes to wonder, but lack tongues to praise.

Sonnet 106   Quotation: *Taming of the Shrew* I ii 142–3

The 'chronicle of wasted time' means the chivalric romances of or about a bygone age. Shakespeare might have thought of Spenser's *Faerie Queene*, set in the youth of King Arthur: it describes paragons of beauty and virtue, and employs the archaic vocabulary copied here in 'wights' (people). A 'blazon' is a poem cataloguing particular beauties. The end couplet concedes the superior beauty of 'old rime', but also has an undercutting lack of enthusiasm to it.

Who will not change a raven for a dove?

O, never say that I was false of heart,
Though absence seemed my flame to qualify;
As easy might I from myself depart
As from my soul, which in thy breast doth lie. 4
That is my home of love: if I have ranged,
Like him that travels I return again,
Just to the time, not with the time exchanged,
So that myself bring water for my stain.   8
Never believe, though in my nature reigned
All frailties that besiege all kinds of blood,
That it could so preposterously be stained
To leave for nothing all thy sum of good;   12
    For nothing this wide universe I call
    Save thou, my rose; in it thou art my all.

Sonnet 109   Quotation: *Midsummer Night's Dream* II ii 114

That the poet has in his turn betrayed the relationship is now apparent. The
lyric opening gets its flow from deploying near clichés, the comparison to a
traveller returning with water to wash off stains of travel pretends to make
tears a total reparation. Some of the vocabulary is latently bawdy; 'preposter-
ously' meant absurdly, perversely, but was also used in the period in the context
of homosexuality, as in 'preposterous venery'.

I can express no kinder sign of love
Than this kind kiss

Alas, 'tis true I have gone here and there
And made myself a motley to the view,
Gored mine own thoughts, sold cheap what is most dear,
Made old offences of affections new.   4
Most true it is that I have looked on truth
Askance and strangely; but, by all above,
These blenches gave my heart another youth,
And worse essays proved thee my best of love.   8
Now all is done, have what shall have no end:
Mine appetite I never more will grind
On newer proof, to try an older friend,
A god in love, to whom I am confined.   12
    Then give me welcome, next my heaven the best,
    Even to thy pure and most most loving breast.

Sonnet 110   Quotation: *Henry VI* Part 2 I i 18–19

The poet has betrayed something precious, and expresses an obscure sense of
self-pollution, which may be linked to his profession ('motley to the view' hints
at the theatre) or to habitual infidelity (l.4). But he swears (l.7) that these
'blenches' (swervings, or glancings aside) rejuvenated his 'heart' (love/
affection), by proving his old love best. But 'confined' (l.12) seems unelated
about the discovery.

O sweet-suggesting love

O, for my sake do you with Fortune chide,
The guilty goddess of my harmful deeds,
That did not better for my life provide
Than public means which public manners breeds.   4
Thence comes it that my name receives a brand;
And almost thence my nature is subdued
To what it works in, like the dyer's hand:
Pity me then, and wish I were renewed,   8
Whilst, like a willing patient, I will drink
Potions of eisell 'gainst my strong infection;
No bitterness that I will bitter think,
Nor double penance, to correct correction.   12
    Pity me then, dear friend, and I assure ye
    Even that your pity is enough to cure me.

Sonnet 111   Quotation: *Two Gentlemen* II vi 7

Infidelity disappears (cf. 110), and here the poet blames the fortune which condemned him to public life in an unesteemed profession. 'Eisel' (l.10) is vinegar; in l.12 a single penance would be 'correction', so an unresented 'double penance' would improve on that. But the couplet requests an easier course: this biographically fascinating sonnet is deeply evasive.

You must not put another scandal on him
That he is open to incontinency

Your love and pity doth th' impression fill
Which vulgar scandal stamped upon my brow;
For what care I who calls me well or ill,
So you o'ergreen my bad, my good allow?   4
You are my all the world, and I must strive
To know my shames and praises from your tongue;
None else to me, nor I to none alive,
That my steeled sense or changes right or wrong.   8
In so profound abysm I throw all care
Of others' voices that my adder's sense
To critic and to flatterer stoppèd are;
Mark how with my neglect I do dispence: 12
    You are so strongly in my purpose bred
    That all the world besides me thinks y'are dead.

Sonnet 112   Quotation: *Hamlet* II i 29–30

The Quarto text reading of l.14, which generally is emended to 'methinks
they're dead' (or similar), is restored here: otherwise the poem ends with a
repetition of the sense of l.7. The poem continues from 111. Line 8: the poet
has hardened himself ('steeled') against the world's opinions, which cannot
alter his own; adders (l.10) were supposed deaf, or capable of stopping their
hearing; 'dispence' (l.12) – account for, explain his neglect of 'others' voices',
a world apparently capable of forgetting the existence of the friend (whom the
sonnet makes a total claim to).

Nature is fine in love, and where 'tis fine
It sends some precious instance of itself
After the thing it loves

Those lines that I before have writ do lie,
Even those that said I could not love you dearer;
Yet then my judgment knew no reason why
My most full flame should afterwards burn clearer.   4
But reckoning Time, whose millioned accidents
Creep in 'twixt vows and change decrees of kings,
Tan sacred beauty, blunt the sharp'st intents,
Divert strong minds to th' course of alt'ring things –   8
Alas, why, fearing of Time's tyranny,
Might I not then say, 'Now I love you best'
When I was certain o'er incertainty,
Crowning the present, doubting of the rest?   12
    Love is a babe; then might I not say so,
     To give full growth to that which still doth grow.

Sonnet 115   Quotation: *Hamlet* IV v 158–60

This sonnet has all the uncertainties 116 excludes: it tries to imagine a non-detrimental effect of Time, ie. that love can grow with Time, so back 'then' (l.13) he could not correctly have said 'Now I love you best'. But the second quatrain surges into the poem with Time's power to degrade and spoil. What he could have said in the past to crown the moment, despite his fear of Time, has (because love has grown) become invalid: but this state also makes it impossible to crown any present with the declaration, so the poem sounds rueful at not having said what it says would have been a lie to say.

Love's not love
When it is mingled with regards that stands
Aloof from th'entire point

Let me not to the marriage of true minds
Admit impediments; love is not love
Which alters when it alteration finds
Or bends with the remover to remove.   4
O, no, it is an ever-fixèd mark
That looks on tempests and is never shaken;
It is the star to every wand'ring bark,
Whose worth's unknown, although his height be taken. 8
Love's not Time's fool, though rosy lips and cheeks
Within his bending sickle's compass come;
Love alters not with his brief hours and weeks,
But bears it out even to the edge of doom.   12
        If this be error, and upon me proved,
        I never writ, nor no man ever loved.

Sonnet 116   Quotation: *King Lear* I i 238–40

The poem shuts out the tribulations of 115, to make a glorious assertion of
unchanging love. The ideal of love sunders it from ordinary life: a sea-mark or
navigator's star (the astral 'worth' or influence of a star, its essential nature,
might be unknown, but the star still be used in ascertaining longitude). Any
particular emphasis of stress in l.1 alters the sense: try the permutations of *me*
or *marriage* or *true minds* or *marriage-of-true-minds*.

My love to thee is sound, sans crack or flaw

Accuse me thus, that I have scanted all
Wherein I should your great deserts repay;
Forgot upon your dearest love to call,
Whereto all bonds do tie me day by day;   4
That I have frequent been with unknown minds
And given to time your own dear-purchased right;
That I have hoisted sail to all the winds
Which should transport me farthest from your sight. 8
Book both my wilfulness and errors down,
And on just proof surmise accumulate;
Bring me within the level of your frown,
But shoot not at me in your wakened hate: 12
    Since my appeal says I did strive to prove
    The constancy and virtue of your love.

Sonnet 117   Quotation: *Love's Labour's Lost* V ii 415

This capricious poem makes self-condemnation sound like boasting (those 'unknown minds' sound intellectually interesting), while constancy to 'your dearest love' is a matter of 'bonds'. The challenge in the third quatrain, particularly l.10, and the audacious flimsiness of the excuse in the final couplet have the effect of not caring what the friend thinks. A very ironic successor to 116.

You may think my love was crafty love

Like as to make our appetites more keen,
With eager compounds we our palate urge;
As to prevent our maladies unseen,
We sicken to shun sickness when we purge: 4
Even so, being full of your ne'er-cloying sweetness,
To bitter sauces did I frame my feeding;
And, sick of welfare, found a kind of meetness
To be diseased ere that there was true needing.   8
Thus policy in love, t'anticipate
The ills that were not, grew to faults assured,
And brought to medicine a healthful state
Which, rank of goodness, would by ill be cured.   12
    But thence I learn, and find the lesson true,
    Drugs poison him that so fell sick of you.

Sonnet 118   Quotation: *King John* IV i 53

The poem, which expands on 111, attempts to account for the poet's behaviour
by an analogy with preventive medicine, the 'eager compounds' (pungent
sauces) of l.2 anticipating the figure if read as 'searching potions'. Purgatives
and bleeding were major recourses of medicine, the old medical notion of a
'plethora' underlies ll.11–12: being sick through overhealth, or 'fullness of the
blood'. 'Love-sick' is the main sense of 'so fell sick of', but Shakespeare also used
the expression in its common modern sense.

I *will be horribly in love with her*

What potions have I drunk of Siren tears
Distilled from limbecks foul as hell within,
Applying fears to hopes and hopes to fears,
Still losing when I saw myself to win!   4
What wretched errors hath my heart committed
Whilst it hath thought itself so blessèd never!
How have mine eyes out of their spheres been fitted
In the distraction of this madding fever!   8
O benefit of ill: now I find true
That better is by evil still made better;
And ruined love, when it is built anew,
Grows fairer than at first, more strong, far greater.   12
    So I return rebuked to my content,
    And gain by ills thrice more than I have spent.

Sonnet 119   Quotation: *Much Ado* II iii 191

It is hard not to suspect this sonnet as deliberately or inadvertently capturing self-dramatisation, so easy is the transition from exclamatory anguish to a complacent 'all for the best' conclusion. 'Limbecks' (l.2) – stills; 'fitted' (l.7) – driven by fits; l.10 expands on 'benefit of ill' – good is enhanced when an evil has been experienced.

Love sought is good, but given unsought is better

That you were once unkind befriends me now,
And for that sorrow which I then did feel
Needs must I under my transgression bow,
Unless my nerves were brass or hammered steel.   4
For if you were by my unkindness shaken,
As I by yours, you've passed a hell of time,
And I, a tyrant, have no leisure taken
To weigh how once I suffered in your crime.   8
O that our night of woe might have rememb'red
My deepest sense how hard true sorrow hits,
And soon to you, as you to me then, tend'red
The humble salve which wounded bosoms fits!   12
   But that your trespass now becomes a fee;
   Mine ransoms yours, and yours must ransom me.

Sonnet 120   Quotation: *Twelfth Night* III i 153

Trying to make himself feel guilty, the poet is here more effective in reminding the friend of his guilt; the main impression is of the poet's former suffering. In inventing feelings for the young man, the poem has to use 'if'. The sense of ll.9–10 is a wish that their recent period of trouble might have brought back to the poet's mind his deepest sense of 'how hard true sorrow hits'.

Love's reason's without reason

'Tis better to be vile than vile esteemed
When not to be receives reproach of being,
And the just pleasure lost, which is so deemed
Not by our feeling but by others' seeing.   4
For why should others' false adulterate eyes
Give salutation to my sportive blood?
Or on my frailties why are frailer spies,
Which in their wills count bad what I think good?   8
No, I am that I am; and they that level
At my abuses reckon up their own:
I may be straight though they themselves be bevel;
By their rank thoughts my deeds must not be shown, 12
    Unless this general evil they maintain:
    All men are bad and in their badness reign.

Sonnet 121   Quotation: *Cymbeline* IV ii 22

Compare 112; another poem in which the poet sets himself above common judgments. 'Vile' retains more of its earliest sense, 'base'; the deeming of l.3–4 is the at-a-glance judgment of the world, judging by its own standards, that one is vile, so robbing one of 'just pleasure'. 'I am that I am' stems from God's words to Moses in *Exodus* 3.14, but versions had appeared in poetry before, eg. Wyatt's poem beginning 'I am as I am'. The sentiment of ll.13–14 is based on the idea that men only prosper ('reign') in life or love through 'badness'.

*When we vow to weep seas, live in fire, eat rocks, tame
    tigers*

> No, Time, thou shalt not boast that I do change:
> Thy pyramids built up with newer might
> To me are nothing novel, nothing strange;
> They are but dressings of a former sight.   4
> Our dates are brief, and therefore we admire
> What thou dost foist upon us that is old,
> And rather make them born to our desire
> Than think that we before have heard them told. 8
> Thy registers and thee I both defy,
> Not wond'ring at the present nor the past;
> For thy records and what we see doth lie,
> Made more or less by thy continual haste.   12
>   This I do vow, and this shall ever be:
>   I will be true, despite thy scythe and thee.

Sonnet 123   Quotation: *Troilus and Cressida* III ii 72–3

The latter poems of the young man sequence return to sublime assertion: here, the records of Time and 'what we see' in the present are dismissed as falsifications: if the span of human life were long enough, the changes brought about by Time would be seen as eternal recurrence. The truth of the poet will abide.

Hang there, my verse, in witness of my love

If my dear love were but the child of state,
It might for Fortune's bastard be unfathered,
As subject to Time's love or to Time's hate,
Weeds among weeds, or flowers with flowers gathered. 4
No, it was builded far from accident;
It suffers not in smiling pomp, nor falls
Under the blow of thrallèd discontent,
Whereto th' inviting time our fashion calls: 8
It fears not Policy, that heretic
Which works on leases of short-numb'red hours,
But all alone stands hugely politic,
That it nor grows with heat nor drowns with show'rs. 12
    To this I witness call the fools of Time,
    Which die for goodness, who have lived for crime.

Sonnet 124   Quotation: *As You Like It* III ii 1

The poet's 'dear love' is finally separated from the young man and identified exclusively with the poet's deepest emotion: 'It might', not 'He might'. It stands apart from the effects both of Time and 'th'inviting time' (the times the poet lives through), while 'the fools of Time', however morally evasive their lives, will finally be fatally embroiled. They can best witness how 'hugely politic' is this indestructible love. Compare this final assertion with 116, and contrast with number 66.

The Rape of Lucrece: extracts

Lucrece, the 'graver labour' Shakespeare had promised Southampton in his dedication of *Venus and Adonis*, appeared in 1594, and went through 6 editions in the poet's lifetime. The narrative is based on Ovid's *Fasti*. It conforms in large part to the 'complaint' genre, in which a wronged person (or their ghost) gives vent to their grief.

Tarquin, King of Rome, is moved to his crime when the husband of Lucrece boasts of her beauty and virtue: leaving their military camp, he goes as a guest bringing news to Lucrece's house. Despising his crime even before he commits it, that night he rapes her. Lucrece sends for her husband, and concentrates and controls her grief by contemplating a depiction of the fall of Troy. In the morning, when her husband arrives, she tells what has happened, and commits suicide. Tarquin and his family are driven from Rome, and a republic established.

Extract one (lines 176–217, one stanza omitted)

> His falchion on a flint he softly smiteth,
> That from the cold stone sparks of fire do fly;
> Whereat a waxen torch forthwith he lighteth,
> Which must be lodestar to his lustful eye;
> And to the flame thus speaks advisedly: 180
>   'As from this cold flint I enforced this fire,
>   So Lucrece must I force to my desire.'
>
> Here pale with fear he doth premeditate
> The dangers of his loathsome enterprise,
> And in his inward mind he doth debate
> What following sorrow may on this arise;
> Then looking scornfully, he doth despise
>   His naked armor of still-slaughterèd lust
>   And justly thus controls his thoughts unjust:

'Fair torch, burn out thy light, and lend it not   190
To darken her whose light excelleth thine;
And die, unhallowed thoughts, before you blot
With your uncleanness that which is divine.
Offer pure incense to so pure a shrine.
    Let fair humanity abhor the deed
    That spots and stains love's modest snow-white weed.

'O shame to knighthood and to shining arms!
O foul dishonor to my household's grave!
O impious act including all foul harms!
A martial man to be soft fancy's slave!   200
True valor still a true respect should have;
    Then my digression is so vile, so base,
    That it will live engraven in my face.

                    (ll.204–10 omitted)

'What win I if I gain the thing I seek?
A dream, a breath, a froth of fleeting joy.
Who buys a minute's mirth to wail a week?
Or sells eternity to get a toy?
For one sweet grape who will the vine destroy?
    Or what fond beggar, but to touch the crown,
    Would with the sceptre straight be stroken down?

Extract two (lines 246–80)

    Thus graceless holds he disputation
    'Tween frozen conscience and hot-burning will,
    And with good thoughts makes dispensation,
    Urging the worser sense for vantage still;
    Which in a moment doth confound and kill   250
        All pure effects, and doth so far proceed
        That what is vile shows like a virtuous deed.

Quoth he, 'She took me kindly by the hand
And gazed for tidings in my eager eyes,
Fearing some hard news from the warlike band
Where her belovèd Collatinus lies.
O, how her fear did make her colour rise!
    First red as roses that on lawn we lay,
    Then white as lawn, the roses took away.

'And how her hand, in my hand being locked,   260
Forced it to tremble with her loyal fear!
Which struck her sad, and then it faster rocked
Until her husband's welfare she did hear;
Whereat she smilèd with so sweet a cheer
    That, had Narcissus seen her as she stood,
    Self-love had never drowned him in the flood.

'Why hunt I then for color or excuses?
All orators are dumb when beauty pleadeth;
Poor wretches have remorse in poor abuses;
Love thrives not in the heart that shadows dreadeth. 270
Affection is my captain, and he leadeth;
    And when his gaudy banner is displayed,
    The coward fights and will not be dismayed.

'Then childish fear avaunt, debating die!
Respect and reason wait on wrinkled age!
My heart shall never countermand mine eye.
Sad pause and deep regard beseems the sage;
My part is youth, and beats these from the stage.
    Desire my pilot is, beauty my prize;
    Then who fears sinking where such treasure lies?' 280

Extract three (lines 470–504)

First like a trumpet doth his tongue begin
To sound a parley to his heartless foe;
Who o'er the white sheet peers her whiter chin,
The reason of this rash alarm to know,
Which he by dumb demeanor seeks to show;
  But she with vehement prayers urgeth still
  Under what colour he commits this ill.

Thus he replies: 'The colour in thy face,
That even for anger makes the lily pale
And the red rose blush at her own disgrace,
Shall plead for me and tell my loving tale.   480
Under that colour am I come to scale
  Thy never-conquerèd fort. The fault is thine,
  For those thine eyes betray thee unto mine.

'Thus I forestall thee, if thou mean to chide:
Thy beauty hath ensnared thee to this night,
Where thou with patience must my will abide,
My will that marks thee for my earth's delight,
Which I to conquer sought with all my might;
  But as reproof and reason beat it dead,
  By thy bright beauty was it newly bred.   490

'I see what crosses my attempt will bring,
I know what thorns the growing rose defends,
I think the honey guarded with a sting;
All this beforehand counsel comprehends,
But Will is deaf and hears no heedful friends:
  Only he hath an eye to gaze on Beauty,
  And dotes on what he looks, 'gainst law or duty.

'I have debated even in my soul
What wrong, what shame, what sorrow I shall breed;
But nothing can affection's course control   500
Or stop the headlong fury of his speed.
I know repentant tears ensue the deed,
    Reproach, disdain, and deadly enmity;
    Yet strive I to embrace mine infamy.'

Extract one   l.176 'falchion' – curved sword; l.179 'lodestar' – guiding star; l.180 'advisedly' – thoughtfully; l.188 'naked armour' – an oxymoron: lust, which dies in its own act, is his armour, his other armour being removed; l.189 'controls' – reproves; l.196 'weed' – clothing ('love's modest snow-white weed' is chastity); l.202 'digression' – deviation from right.

Extract two   l.248 'makes dispensation' – does away with; l.251 'effects' – desires; ll.258–9 'lawn' – linen; l.267 'colour' – pretext; l.276 'heart' – for deeper feelings; at l.200 he terms his desire 'Fancy', the emphasis is on his 'eye' (compare 'Tell me where is fancy bred' p.19), 'countermand' – contradict.

Extract three   l.471 'sound a parley' – summon defenders to negotiation, 'heartless' – terrified; ll.475–7–81 'colour' puns on 'pretext', 'hue' and 'banner'; l.502 'ensue' – follow on.

'The Phoenix and Turtle'

Written about the time that Shakespeare wrote *Hamlet*, and when, as we see from p.29, Shakespeare was toying with 'metaphysical' poetry, the poem we call 'The Phoenix and Turtle', just as the play makes new an older genre (the revenge play), takes traditional material and makes something radically new. An assembly of the birds is lifted into levels of abstraction which amply qualified the poem, as the volume in which it appeared boasted, as being by 'the best and chiefest of our moderne writers'. Like *Hamlet*, too, is the way that a modern, subtle and captivating intellect mourns the departure of grandeur, simplicity, value. The total effect is 'remote, yet not asunder'. It must always have been a difficult poem: words invented for the poem include 'precurrer', 'defunctive', 'distincts', there are the unusual compounds 'death-divining', 'treble-dated', 'co-supremes', and Shakespeare uses only here 'concordant', 'interdict' and the singular form 'obsequy', while 'THRENOS' is an example of Shakespeare's 'small *Latine* and lesse *Greeke*'. Nevertheless, 'O twas a moving Epicedium!' wrote Marston, the next poet in the volume, and for many subsequent readers, this celebration of perfect love departed in a 'mutual flame' has a strange incantatory power, like the other recitations Shakespeare wrote in seven syllable lines, the closing speeches in *A Midsummer Night's Dream* and *The Tempest*.

> Let the bird of loudest lay
> On the sole Arabian tree
> Herald sad and trumpet be,
> To whose sound chaste wings obey.
>
> But thou shrieking harbinger,
> Foul precurrer of the fiend,
> Augur of the fever's end,
> To this troop come thou not near.

From this session interdict
Every fowl of tyrant wing,   10
Save the eagle, feath'red king:
Keep the obsequy so strict.

Let the priest in surplice white,
That defunctive music can,
Be the death-divining swan,
Lest the requiem lack his right.

And thou treble-dated crow,
That thy sable gender mak'st
With the breath thou giv'st and tak'st,
'Mongst our mourners shalt thou go.   20

Here the anthem doth commence:
Love and constancy is dead,
Phoenix and the turtle fled
In a mutual flame from hence.

So they loved as love in twain
Had the essence but in one;
Two distincts, division none:
Number there in love was slain.

Hearts remote, yet not asunder;
Distance, and no space was seen   30
'Twixt this turtle and his queen;
But in them it were a wonder.

So between them love did shine
That the turtle saw his right
Flaming in the phoenix' sight:
Either was the other's mine.

Property was thus appallèd,
That the self was not the same;
Single nature's double name
Neither two nor one was callèd.   40

Reason, in itself confounded,
Saw division grow together,
To themselves yet either neither,
Simple were so well compounded;

That it cried, 'How true a twain
Seemeth this concordant one!
Love hath reason, reason none,
If what parts can so remain.'

Whereupon it made this threne
To the phoenix and the dove,   50
Co-supremes and stars of love,
As chorus to their tragic scene.

THRENOS

Beauty, truth, and rarity,
Grace in all simplicity,
Here enclosed, in cinders lie.

Death is now the phoenix' nest;
And the turtle's loyal breast
To eternity doth rest,

Leaving no posterity:
'Twas not their infirmity,   60
It was married chastity.

Truth may seem, but cannot be;
Beauty brag, but 'tis not she:
Truth and Beauty buried be.

To this urn let those repair
That are either true or fair;
For these dead birds sigh a prayer.

Published without title in Robert Chester's *Loves Martyr* (1601), with poems by other poets all thematically linked to the Phoenix myth. Shakespeare chose to ignore both the apparent occasion (his birds leave 'no posterity', Chester's patron hadn't died, and had ten children) and the myth (instead of regenerating from the ashes of its funeral pyre, the phoenix dies).

Title: the 'turtle', the male in this perfect union, is of course the turtle dove, the bird being a symbol of constancy in love. Lines 1–20 – use the medieval device of an assembly of the birds, here for a funeral procession; l.1 – the bird with the loudest 'lay' might be the nightingale; l.5 'harbinger' – the screech owl, whose cry augurs a death; l.10 'fowl of tyrant wing' – birds of prey; ll.13–15 allude to the story that swans sing only when about to die; l.16 'his right' – what is due to it, 'proper rites'; ll.17–19 allude to beliefs that crows lived up to 400 years, and attaches a piece of lore about ravens, that they engendered at the beak. Lines 21–52 The Anthem: a series of metaphysical conceits on two becoming one, so that (l.28) 'number . . . was slain'; l.36 'mine': either as in Sonnet 134 l.3, the other possessed as completely as the self, or source of wealth, as in 'O Antony, thou mine of bounty!'; l.44 turns on the difference between a 'simple' (one ingredient) and a 'compound' as in medicinal drugs; 'threne' – a threnody, funeral song.

Sonnets: The Dark Lady

Well, I will love, write, sigh, pray, sue and groan
Some men must love my Lady, and some Joan

In the old age black was not counted fair,
Or, if it were, it bore not beauty's name;
But now is black beauty's successive heir,
And beauty slandered with a bastard shame;   4
For since each hand hath put on nature's power,
Fairing the foul with art's false borrowed face,
Sweet beauty hath no name, no holy bower,
But is profaned, if not lives in disgrace.   8
Therefore my mistress' brows are raven black,
Her eyes so suited, and they mourners seem
At such who, not born fair, no beauty lack,
Sland'ring creation with a false esteem: 12
  Yet so they mourn, becoming of their woe,
  That every tongue says beauty should look so.

Sonnet 127   Quotation: *Love's Labour's Lost* III i 194–5

The conceit of the poem is that the dark eyes and brows of the Lady are a form
of mourning at the prevalence of merely cosmetic beauty. Lines 3–4 black is
now heir to beauty, as fair 'beauty' is declared illegitimate; ll.7–8 what was
formerly worshipped is now profaned.

Sing, boy; my spirit grows heavy in love

How oft, when thou, my music, music play'st
Upon that blessèd wood whose motion sounds
With thy sweet fingers when thou gently sway'st
The wiry concord that mine ear confounds,   4
Do I envy those jacks that nimble leap
To kiss the tender inward of thy hand,
Whilst my poor lips, which should that harvest reap,
At the wood's boldness by thee blushing stand.   8
To be so tickled they would change their state
And situation with those dancing chips
O'er whom thy fingers walk with gentle gait,
Making dead wood more blest than living lips.   12
    Since saucy jacks so happy are in this,
    Give them thy fingers, me thy lips to kiss.

Sonnet 128   Quotation: *Love's Labour's Lost* I ii 117

One of many sonnets in the period expressing the desire for erotic self-transformation, to get into contact with the lady. Here she is playing a keyboard instrument. Shakespeare avails himself of the term 'jacks' (properly the parts which plucked the strings) for the whole action of the virginals, so as to activate the personification of the keys as his envied rivals.

the desire is boundless and the act a slave to limit

Th' expense of spirit in a waste of shame
Is lust in action; and, till action, lust
Is perjured, murd'rous, bloody, full of blame,
Savage, extreme, rude, cruel, not to trust;   4
Enjoyed no sooner but despisèd straight;
Past reason hunted, and no sooner had,
Past reason hated as a swallowed bait
On purpose laid to make the taker mad: 8
Mad in pursuit, and in possession so;
Had, having, and in quest to have, extreme;
A bliss in proof, and proved, a very woe;
Before, a joy proposed; behind, a dream.   12
    All this the world well knows; yet none knows well
    To shun the heaven that leads men to this hell.

Sonnet 129   Quotation: *Troilus and Cressida* III ii 77–8

This famous sonnet anticipates the syntactical effects of Milton's sonnets: the energy of the syntax threatens to burst the formal bounds of the sonnet form. The denunciation of lust (and 'spirit' in l.1 could mean 'semen') nevertheless can acknowledge 'A bliss in proof' in lust. Lines 7–8 resemble Fulke Greville's *Caelica*, Poem 83, 'I swallow downe the baite, which carries down my death', or *Measure for Measure* I ii 124–6.

My love is most immaculate white and red

My mistress' eyes are nothing like the sun;
Coral is far more red than her lips' red;
If snow be white, why then her breasts are dun;
If hairs be wires, black wires grow on her head. 4
I have seen roses damasked, red and white,
But no such roses see I in her cheeks;
And in some perfumes is there more delight
Than in the breath that from my mistress reeks. 8
I love to hear her speak; yet well I know
That music hath a far more pleasing sound:
I grant I never saw a goddess go;
My mistress, when she walks, treads on the ground. 12
    And yet, by heaven, I think my love as rare
    As any she belied with false compare.

Sonnet 130   Quotation: *Love's Labour's Lost* I ii 88

The sonnet discovers that there is space to praise the mistress this side of the hyperbolic affirmations of conventional sonneteers. All the comparisons rejected in the poem can be found in Elizabethan sonnet writing, and, indeed, elsewhere in Shakespeare. The word 'reeks' in l.8 was not used in association with bad smells till the 18th century. The cheery levity of this sonnet soon sours into poems about the woman's physical and moral ugliness.

Take it, and hit
The innocent mansion of my love, my heart

Thou art as tyrannous, so as thou art,
As those whose beauties proudly make them cruel;
For well thou know'st to my dear, doting heart
Thou art the fairest and most precious jewel.   4
Yet, in good faith, some say that thee behold,
Thy face hath not the power to make love groan;
To say they err I dare not be so bold,
Although I swear it to myself alone.   8
And, to be sure that is not false I swear,
A thousand groans, but thinking on thy face,
One on another's neck, do witness bear
Thy black is fairest in my judgment's place.   12
    In nothing art thou black save in thy deeds,
    And thence this slander, as I think, proceeds.

Sonnet 131   Quotation: *Cymbeline* III iv 65–6

The sonnet deals again with the problem of loving a woman whose beauty is
either unfashionable or only in the eyes of the besotted lover. With studied
blandness, the closing couplet makes its own accusation (her black deeds) in
the form of a defence of her fairness (=beauty) against the slanderers of her
looks in ll.5–6. The preoccupation with swearing, vowing what is impossible,
marks this and other sonnets: the poet summons his groans as supporting
witnesses to what only he sees.

Love keeps his revels where there are but twain

Beshrew that heart that makes my heart to groan
For that deep wound it gives my friend and me:
Is't not enough to torture me alone,
But slave to slavery my sweet'st friend must be?   4
Me from myself thy cruel eye hath taken,
And my next self thou harder hast engrossed;
Of him, myself, and thee I am forsaken,
A torment thrice threefold thus to be crossed.   8
Prison my heart in thy steel bosom's ward,
But then my friend's heart let my poor heart bail;
Whoe'er keeps me, let my heart be his guard:
Thou canst not then use rigor in my jail.   12
    And yet thou wilt; for I, being pent in thee,
    Perforce am thine, and all that is in me.

Sonnet 133   Quotation: *Venus and Adonis* 123

The sonnet apparently reprises Sonnets 41 and 42, but this time addresses the woman. The ideas of imprisonment and torture lead up to the conceit that the poet, having the young man in his heart, cannot save him from the cruelty of the woman, being himself 'pent in thee'. 'Engrossed' in l.6 is a multiple pun: she both fascinates the young man, monopolises him like a merchant controlling all a marketable product, and makes his behaviour gross.

There lives within the very flame of love
A kind of wick or snuff

So, now I have confessed that he is thine
And I myself am mortgaged to thy will,
Myself I'll forfeit, so that other mine
Thou wilt restore to be my comfort still: 4
But thou wilt not, nor he will not be free,
For thou art covetous, and he is kind;
He learned but surety-like to write for me
Under that bond that him as fast doth bind.   8
The statute of thy beauty thou wilt take,
Thou usurer that put'st forth all to use,
And sue a friend came debtor for my sake;
So him I lose through my unkind abuse.   12
     Him have I lost, thou hast both him and me;
     He pays the whole, and yet am I not free.

Sonnet 134   Quotation: *Hamlet* IV vii 114–15

The sense reads on from 133, which was the confession of l.1. Here
Shakespeare thinks of imprisonment for debt: the friend stood surety for the
poet's bond, her covetousness has them both imprisoned, and will not release
the poet despite the friend being adequate payment for the 'whole' (l.14).
There is a bawdy pun here on 'hole', while l.10 accuses the woman of
whoreishness, money lending and prostitution being 'the two usuries' in
contemporary parlance (see *Measure for Measure* III ii 5).

Words, vows, gifts, tears, and love's full sacrifice
He offers

Whoever hath her wish, thou hast thy Will,
And Will to boot, and Will in overplus.
More than enough am I that vex thee still,
To thy sweet will making addition thus.   4
Wilt thou, whose will is large and spacious,
Not once vouchsafe to hide my will in thine?
Shall will in others seem right gracious,
And in my will no fair acceptance shine?   8
The sea, all water, yet receives rain still
And in abundance addeth to his store;
So thou, being rich in Will, add to thy Will
One will of mine to make thy large Will more. 12
    Let no unkind, no fair beseechers kill;
    Think all but one, and me in that one Will.

Sonnet 135   Quotation: *Troilus and Cressida* I ii 274–5

In Sonnets 134, 135 and 143 Shakespeare puns on his own first name, which he shares, apparently, with both his friend and the Dark Lady's husband. 'Will' allows play on the sense, 'what you desire', especially sexually, 'will' serving for both the male and female genitalia. The simple future tense also is played upon, and after the sexual-financial covetousness figure of 134, 'rich in Will' fleetingly suggests 'having a lot to bequeath'. In the couplet, she is asked not to refuse him with an unkind 'no', but accept his 'will' into her 'will' along with her other Wills.

With truant vows to her own lips he loves
And dare avow her beauty

If thy soul check thee that I come so near,
Swear to thy blind soul that I was thy Will,
And will, thy soul knows, is admitted there:
Thus far for love my love-suit, sweet, fulfil.   4
Will will fulfil the treasure of thy love
Ay, fill it full with wills, and my will one.
In things of great receipt with ease we prove
Among a number one is reckoned none.   8
Then in the number let me pass untold,
Though in thy store's account I one must be;
For nothing hold me, so it please thee hold
That nothing me, a something, sweet, to thee.   12
    Make but my name thy love, and love that still,
    And then thou lovest me, for my name is Will.

Sonnet 136   Quotation: *Troilus and Cressida* I iii 270–1

Line 1: 'check' means reprove – the sentiment resembles the maxim in
Overbury's poem, 'A Wife', 'He comes too near that comes to be denied' (ie. to
have to refuse a man shows too much freedom has already been allowed). The
pun on 'Will' allows the woman to pass off 'Will' to her soul as her will. The
arithmetical conceit of ll. 7–12 turns on the insignificance of one among many,
and as in Sonnet 20, makes play between the male 'thing' and female no-thing
(where the poet's thing would be negligible among so many).

Things base and vile, holding no quantity
Love can transpose to form and dignity

Thou blind fool, Love, what dost thou to mine eyes
That they behold and see not what they see?
They know what beauty is, see where it lies,
Yet what the best is take the worst to be.   4
If eyes, corrupt by over-partial looks,
Be anchored in the bay where all men ride,
Why of eyes' falsehood hast thou forgèd hooks,
Whereto the judgment of my heart is tied?   8
Why should my heart think that a several plot
Which my heart knows the wide world's common place?
Or mine eyes seeing this, say this is not,
To put fair truth upon so foul a face?   12
     In things right true my heart and eyes have erred,
     And to this false plague are they now transferred.

Sonnet 137   Quotation: *Midsummer Night's Dream* I i 232-3

After a group of sonnets addressed to the Lady, the poet in anguish here asks Love what he is doing to him. The inability to square what his heart thinks with what it knows recalls Troilus's reaction to the infidelity of Cressida. As free to all men as the sea (but the poet's heart cannot sail away from where it is anchored), or as common ground rather than his own private ('several') plot, the woman induces self-contradiction in which false is taken for true, and foul for fair.

Do not fall in love with me
For I am falser than vows made in wine

When my love swears that she is made of truth
I do believe her, though I know she lies,
That she might think me some untutored youth,
Unlearnèd in the world's false subtilties.   4
Thus vainly thinking that she thinks me young,
Although she knows my days are past the best,
Simply I credit her false-speaking tongue;
On both sides thus is simple truth suppressed.   8
But wherefore says she not she is unjust?
And wherefore say not I that I am old?
O, love's best habit is in seeming trust,
And age in love loves not to have years told.   12
    Therefore I lie with her and she with me,
    And in our faults by lies we flattered be.

Sonnet 138   Quotation: *As You Like It* III v 71–2

In this superlative sonnet, the misrepresentations of both are examined,
No. 137 having been confined to the poet's. A disparity of age has not
previously been an issue. The poem certainly dates from before 1599 (when a
version was published): Shakespeare would have been less than 35. His
receding hair led him to play older men on stage (eg. the father in *Every Man
in his Humour* 1598). The obvious pun on lies (with) in line 13 makes us see
the point of ll.1–2: she is not true to him sexually.

Under love's heavy burden do I sink

Be wise as thou art cruel: do not press
My tongue-tied patience with too much disdain,
Lest sorrow lend me words, and words express
The manner of my pity-wanting pain.   4
If I might teach thee wit, better it were,
Though not to love, yet, love, to tell me so;
As testy sick men, when their deaths be near,
No news but health from their physicians know.   8
For if I should despair, I should grow mad,
And in my madness might speak ill of thee:
Now this ill-wresting world is grown so bad
Mad slanderers by mad ears believèd be.   12
     That I may not be so, nor thou belied,
     Bear thine eyes straight, though thy proud heart go wide.

Sonnet 140   Quotation: *Romeo and Juliet* I iv 22

In l.6, understand 'Though you don't love me, tell me you do'. The sonnet
threatens outspokenness while being so. Editors point out that l.14 uses a
figure from archery: her eyes should aim straight at him, even if her heart flies
wide. 'Proud' there refers to her disdain in l.2, but Elizabethans could also use
the word for 'aroused' (see Spenser, *The Faerie Queene* III xi 39 and sonnet
151).

Didst thou but know the inly touch of love

In faith, I do not love thee with mine eyes,
For they in thee a thousand errors note;
But 'tis my heart that loves what they despise,
Who in despite of view is pleased to dote.   4
Nor are mine ears with thy tongue's tune delighted,
Nor tender feeling to base touches prone,
Nor taste, nor smell, desire to be invited
To any sensual feast with thee alone;   8
But my five wits nor my five senses can
Dissuade one foolish heart from serving thee,
Who leaves unswayed the likeness of a man,
Thy proud heart's slave and vassal wretch to be: 12
   Only my plague thus far I count my gain,
   That she that makes me sin awards me pain.

Sonnet 141   Quotation: *Two Gentlemen* II vii 18

The sonnet sums up the thought of several proceeding sonnets (that
objectively the woman's looks do not merit the love, ignoring the evidence of
your own eyes and reason, the 'proud heart' is carried over from 140, 'plague'
from 137), but adding 'sin', the religious term of condemnation missing even
from 129, so projecting us forward to 146. The five wits corresponding to the
five senses were common sense, imagination, fancy, judgment and memory.

Love is like a child,
That longs for everything that he can come by

Lo, as a careful housewife runs to catch
One of her feathered creatures broke away,
Sets down her babe, and makes all swift dispatch
In pursuit of the thing she would have stay;   4
Whilst her neglected child holds her in chase,
Cries to catch her whose busy care is bent
To follow that which flies before her face,
Not prizing her poor infant's discontent: 8
So runn'st thou after that which flies from thee,
Whilst I, thy babe, chase thee afar behind;
But if thou catch thy hope, turn back to me
And play the mother's part, kiss me, be kind.   12
    So will I pray that thou mayst have thy Will,
    If thou turn back and my loud crying still.

Sonnet 143   Quotation: *Two Gentlemen* III i 124–5

The sonnet finds a way to convert the poet into 'thy babe'. In *Venus and Adonis* Shakespeare clearly enjoys putting together the mature female and the boy: Anne Hathaway was eight years older than her husband . . . but the sonnet is deliberately grotesque, making the complex erotic situation into a housewife chasing an escaped hen, ignoring the baby trying to catch her. The familiar pun on 'Will' allows him to wish her success in praying for his own.

Love is a familiar; Love is a devil: there is no evil angel but Love

Two loves I have, of comfort and despair,
Which like two spirits do suggest me still:
The better angel is a man right fair,
The worser spirit a woman colored ill.   4
To win me soon to hell, my female evil
Tempteth my better angel from my side,
And would corrupt my saint to be a devil,
Wooing his purity with her foul pride.   8
And whether that my angel be turned fiend
Suspect I may, yet not directly tell;
But being both from me, both to each friend,
I guess one angel in another's hell.   12
    Yet this shall I ne'er know, but live in doubt,
    Till my bad angel fire my good one out.

Sonnet 144   Quotation: *Love's Labour's Lost* I ii 164–5

Boccaccio (*Decameron* III 10) has a story of a beautiful girl who wanted to become a hermit. She went into the desert for instruction, but the first hermit she met sent her away, fearing her charms. At last, an especially holy hermit undertook to instruct her. But soon even he was full of desire, and told her of his personal devil, which she asked to see. Do I have one? she asks, for she was naive as well as beautiful. No, but you have a hell, he replied. Soon they are busy driving the devil into hell . . .

The expedition of my violent love
Outrun the pauser, reason

Poor soul, the centre of my sinful earth,
[   ] these rebel pow'rs that thee array,
Why dost thou pine within and suffer dearth,
Painting thy outward walls so costly gay?   4
Why so large cost, having so short a lease,
Dost thou upon thy fading mansion spend?
Shall worms, inheritors of this excess,
Eat up thy charge? Is this thy body's end?   8
Then, soul, live thou upon thy servant's loss,
And let that pine to aggravate thy store;
Buy terms divine in selling hours of dross;
Within be fed, without be rich no more: 12
    So shalt thou feed on Death, that feeds on men,
    And Death once dead, there's no more dying then.

Sonnet 146   Quotation: *Macbeth* II iii 109–10

Shakespeare's 'Holy Sonnet', reminiscent of Donne. This meditation on worldly vanity makes no mention of love, but is a product of the moral self-scrutiny the affair has induced. The soul is starving like a besieged town, but spends its stores on exterior vanity. Line 2 is misprinted in the 1609 text: editorial suggestions include 'Spoiled by', 'Starved by', 'Pressed with', 'Fooled by'. The last line echoes several biblical texts, eg. *Revelations* 21.4 'there shall be no more death'.

Thou lay'st in every gash that love hath given me
The knife that made it

My love is as a fever, longing still
For that which longer nurseth the disease,
Feeding on that which doth preserve the ill,
Th' uncertain sickly appetite to please.   4
My reason, the physician to my love,
Angry that his prescriptions are not kept,
Hath left me, and I desperate now approve
Desire is death, which physic did except.   8
Past cure I am, now reason is past care,
And frantic-mad with evermore unrest;
My thoughts and my discourse as madmen's are,
At random from the truth vainly expressed: 12
    For I have sworn thee fair, and thought thee bright,
    Who art as black as hell, as dark as night.

Sonnet 147   Quotation: *Troilus and Cressida* I i 62–3

After the religious moralising of 146, this sonnet develops various conven-
tional or proverbial wisdoms ('starve a fever', reason as cure for passion, 'past
cure past care') and common similes (lines 1, 11 and 14). In l.8, the sense is that
'physic' (reason) prescribed desire. Kerrigan notes 'evermore' (l.10) is both
unceasing and 'ever more', increasing.

Love looks not with the eyes, but with the mind
And therefore is wing'd Cupid painted blind

O, from what pow'r hast thou this pow'rful might
With insufficiency my heart to sway?
To make me give the lie to my true sight
And swear that brightness doth not grace the day?   4
Whence hast thou this becoming of things ill,
That in the very refuse of thy deeds
There is such strength and warrantise of skill
That in my mind thy worst all best exceeds?   8
Who taught thee how to make me love thee more,
The more I hear and see just cause of hate?
O, though I love what others do abhor,
With others thou shouldst not abhor my state: 12
    If thy unworthiness raised love in me,
    More worthy I to be beloved of thee.

Sonnet 150   Quotation: *Midsummer Night's Dream* I i 234-5

The sonnet recollects Enobarbus' inverted compliment to Cleopatra: 'vilest things / Become themselves in her, that the holy priests / Bless her when she is riggish' (ie. randy). In l.2 'insufficiency' – defect, imperfection; 'sway' – rule or 'cause to waver'; l.6 'refuse' – most worthless part (Shakespeare's sole use of the noun); ll.11–12 'abhor' allows a punning coinage, 'ab-whore', 'to make whoreish / behave like a whore'.

therefore is Love said to be a child
Because in choice he is so oft beguil'd

Love is too young to know what conscience is;
Yet who knows not conscience is born of love?
Then, gentle cheater, urge not my amiss,
Lest guilty of my faults thy sweet self prove   4
For, thou betraying me, I do betray
My nobler part to my gross body's treason;
My soul doth tell my body that he may
Triumph in love; flesh stays no farther reason,   8
But, rising at thy name, doth point out thee
As his triumphant prize. Proud of this pride,
He is contented thy poor drudge to be,
To stand in thy affairs, fall by thy side.   12
      No want of conscience hold it that I call
      Her 'love' for whose dear love I rise and fall.

Sonnet 151   Quotation: *Midsummer Night's Dream* I i 238–9

The bawdy in this sonnet is obvious, but the circumstances obscure. The poet
has apparently betrayed the addressee sexually as well as his soul morally. The
couplet, unusually, is a comment aside from the direct address. 'Conscience' has
a latent bawdy sense, 'con' (as in French), plus 'science' as (sexual) knowledge.
There is a lurking figure of the penis as a devil, for conjuring spirits by a name
– see *Julius Caesar* I ii 146–7.

Love bade me swear, and Love bids me forswear

In loving thee thou know'st I am forsworn,
But thou art twice forsworn, to me love swearing;
In act thy bed-vow broke, and new faith torn
In vowing new hate after new love bearing.   4
But why of two oaths' breach do I accuse thee
When I break twenty? I am perjured most,
For all my vows are oaths but to misuse thee,
And all my honest faith in thee is lost;   8
For I have sworn deep oaths of thy deep kindness,
Oaths of thy love, thy truth, thy constancy;
And, to enlighten thee, gave eyes to blindness,
Or made them swear against the thing they see;   12
   For I have sworn thee fair: more perjured eye,
   To swear against the truth so foul a lie.

Sonnet 152   Quotation: *Two Gentlemen* II vi 6

A final intense analysis of all the betrayals their affair has accumulated: the marriage vow, vows to lovers, the oaths made only to deceive, affirmations made in the face of known truth. The Dark Lady remains un-fair, only by wilful blindness can she be 'enlightened' as fair, kind, true, constant, loving. The 'eye-I' pun was a favourite with Shakespeare, and might even suggest the affirmative 'aye'.

The Final Vision:
extracts from *The Two Noble Kinsmen*

At the end of his career, Shakespeare collaborated with John Fletcher
on a dramatisation of Chaucer's *The Knight's Tale*. The play, *The Two
Noble Kinsmen*, was performed in 1613 or early 1614 at the Blackfriars
theatre. The mood of the play, which combines wedding celebrations
and mourning, may have been affected by the death of Prince Henry
late in 1612, which was followed by the marriage of his sister, the
Princess Elizabeth, to Frederick of Bohemia on Valentine's day 1613.

The 'two noble kinsmen' are Thebans called Palamon and Arcite,
who fight reluctantly but bravely in battle against Theseus, Duke of
Athens. Captured and imprisoned, they see Emilia, sister of Theseus's
wife Hippolyta through the window of their cell, and fall in love with
her. Arcite has his liberty procured, and Theseus banishes him from the
kingdom, while Palamon remains. Arcite returns to Athens with
another identity, Palamon is freed by the Jailer's daughter. They meet,
and quarrel, are found fighting: Palamon reveals who they are, and
Theseus finally decides that they must settle their fates by mortal
combat. Arcite prays to Mars for victory, Palamon to Venus, the divided
Emilia to Diana. Both the kinsmen receive favourable signs, and Arcite
defeats Palamon in combat, but expires after his victory: Palamon is
taken from the gallows to be given Emilia's hand in marriage.

In the last plays, there is some evidence of Shakespeare idealising a
pre-sexual love, and depicting in sexual relationships unhappiness or
trauma (jealousy in *The Winter's Tale*, incest in Antiochus and his
daughter in *Pericles*). There is a marked concern in *The Tempest* and
Cymbeline with pre-nuptial chastity.

In the three following extracts, Emilia speaks of her love for her dead
playmate Flavina, Arcite rhapsodises on being in prison with his friend
Palamon as a perfect existence, and, finally, Palamon prays to Venus.
The speech by Arcite is assigned by some authorities to Shakespeare's
collaborator, Fletcher, but is like Polixenes' speech in *The Winter's
Tale* I ii 67-75.

Extract one

EMILIA   I was acquainted
  Once with a time when I enjoyed a playfellow;   50
  You were at wars when she the grave enriched,
  Who made too proud the bed; took leave o'th' moon –
  Which then looked pale at parting – when our count
  Was each eleven.
HIPPOLYTA   'Twas Flavina.
EMILIA   Yes.
  You talk of Pirithous' and Theseus' love:
  Theirs has more ground, is more maturely seasoned,
  More buckled with strong judgement, and their needs
  The one of th'other may be said to water
  Their intertangled roots of love; but I
  And she I sigh and spoke of were things innocent,   60
  Loved for we did, and like the elements,
  That know not what, nor why, yet do effect
  Rare issues by their operance, our souls
  Did so to one another. What she liked
  Was then of me approved; what not, condemned –
  No more arraignment. The flower that I would pluck
  And put between my breasts – O then but beginning
  To swell about the blossom – she would long
  Till she had such another, and commit it
  To the like innocent cradle, where, phoenix-like,   70
  They died in perfume. On my head no toy
  But was her pattern. Her affections – pretty,
  Though happily her careless wear – I followed
  For my most serious decking. Had mine ear
  Stol'n some new air, or at adventure hummed one,
  From musical coinage, why, it was a note
  Whereon her spirits would sojourn – rather dwell on –
  And sing it in her slumbers. This rehearsal –
  Which, seely innocence wots well, comes in

Like old emportment's bastard – has this end: 80
That the true love 'tween maid and maid may be
More than in sex dividual.

                    (I iii 49–82)

Extract two

ARCITE
  Shall we make worthy uses of this place
  That all men hate so much?
PALAMON   How, gentle cousin?   70
ARCITE
  Let's think this prison holy sanctuary,
  To keep us from corruption of worse men.
  We are young, and yet desire the ways of honour
  That liberty and common conversation,
  The poison of pure spirits, might, like women,
  Woo us to wander from. What worthy blessing
  Can be, but our imaginations
  May make it ours? And here being thus together,
  We are an endless mine to one another:
  We are one another's wife, ever begetting   80
  New births of love; we are father, friends, acquaintance;
  We are in one another, families –
  I am your heir, and you are mine; this place
  Is our inheritance: no hard oppressor
  Dare take this from us. Here, with a little patience,
  We shall live long and loving. No surfeits seek us –
  The hand of war hurts none here, nor the seas
  Swallow their youth. Were we at liberty
  A wife might part us lawfully, or business;
  Quarrels consume us; envy of ill men   90
  Crave our acquaintance. I might sicken, cousin,
  Where you should never know it, and so perish

Without your noble hand to close mine eyes,
Or prayers to the gods. A thousand chances,
Were we from hence, would sever us.

PALAMON   You have made me –
I thank you, cousin Arcite – almost wanton
With my captivity.

                              (II ii 69–97)

Extract three

PALAMON   To the goddess Venus
Commend we our proceeding, and implore
Her power unto our party.
          *Here they kneel before the altar, [fall on their faces then
          on their knees again]*
(*Praying to Venus*) Hail, sovereign queen of secrets, who hast
     power
To call the fiercest tyrant from his rage
And weep unto a girl; that hast the might,
Even with an eye-glance, to choke Mars's drum   80
And turn th'alarum to whispers; that canst make
A cripple flourish with his crutch, and cure him
Before Apollo; that mayst force the king
To be his subject's vassal, and induce
Stale gravity to dance; the polled bachelor
Whose youth, like wanton boys through bonfires,
Have skipped thy flame, at seventy thou canst catch
And make him to the scorn of his hoarse throat
Abuse young lays of love. What godlike power
Hast thou not power upon? To Phoebus thou   90
Add'st flames hotter than his – the heavenly fires
Did scorch his mortal son, thine him. The huntress,
All moist and cold, some say, began to throw
Her bow away and sigh. Take to thy grace
Me, thy vowed soldier, who do bear thy yoke
As 'twere a wreath of roses, yet is heavier

Than lead itself, stings more than nettles.
I have never been foul-mouthed against thy law;
Ne'er revealed secret, for I knew none; would not,
Had I kenned all that were. I never practised   100
Upon man's wife, nor would the libels read
Of liberal wits. I never at great feasts
Sought to betray a beauty, but have blushed
At simp'ring sirs that did. I have been harsh
To large confessors, and have hotly asked them
If they had mothers – I had one, a woman,
And women 'twere they wronged. I knew a man
Of eighty winters, this I told them, who
A lass of fourteen brided – 'twas thy power
To put life into dust. The agèd cramp   110
Had screwed his square foot round,
The gout had knit his fingers into knots,
Torturing convulsions from his globy eyes
Had almost drawn their spheres, that what was life
In him seemed torture. This anatomy
Had by his young fair fere a boy, and I
Believed it was his, for she swore it was,
And who would not believe her? Brief – I am
To those that prate and have done, no companion;
To those that boast and have not, a defier;   120
To those that would and cannot, a rejoicer.
Yea, him I do not love that tells close offices
The foulest way, nor names concealments in
The boldest language. Such a one I am,
And vow that lover never yet made sigh
Truer than I. O, then, most soft sweet goddess,
Give me the victory of this question, which
Is true love's merit, and bless me with a sign
Of thy great pleasure.
     Here music is heard, doves are seen to flutter. They fall
          again upon their faces, then on their knees
O thou that from eleven to ninety reign'st   130
In mortal bosoms, whose chase is this world

And we in herds thy game, I give thee thanks
For this fair token, which, being laid unto
Mine innocent true heart, arms in assurance
My body to this business. (*To his Knights*) Let us rise
And bow before the goddess.
  They rise and bow
        Time comes on.   *Exeunt*

    (V i 74–136)

Extract one   l.52 'took leave o'the'moon' – died (the moon being Diana); l.63 'operance' – operation; l.66 'arraignment' – formal accusation; l.71 'toy' – ornament; ll.72–4 – the things she wore (ie. 'affected') were pretty even if casually put on, I followed them when dressing carefully; l.75 'air' – tune; l.78 'rehearsal' – account I'm giving; l.80 'emportment' – passion. The sense of the lines is that 'seely' (happy) innocence knows these things well, my account is a poor representation of the former passion.

Extract two   l.79 'mine' – source of wealth; l.86 'surfeits' – excesses; ll.90–1 the sense appears to be, ill (evil) men, in envy of us, will crave our acquaintance (so spoiling our mutuality).

Extract three   Palamon is accompanied by the three knights who will fight with him. Line 83 Apollo was the God of healing; l.85 'polled' – bald; l.92 Phaethon was Phoebus' 'mortal son'; l.100 'kenned' – known; l.102 'liberal' – licentious; l.105 'large confessors' – men who brag of their sexual conquests; l.111 'square' – ie. arthritic, swollen; l.115 'anatomy' – skeleton; l.116 'fere' – mate; l.119 'prate and have done' – done what they boast of; ll.122–3 'close offices ... concealments' – affairs of Venus, 'queene of secrets'; l.131 'chase' – hunting ground.

INDEX OF FIRST LINES TO SONNETS AND SONGS